D0041137

THE
FOUR
SPIRITUAL
LAWS
OF
PROSPERITY

A Simple Guide to
Unlimited Abundance

EDWENE GAINES

RODALE

© 2005 by Edwene Gaines

Cover illustration © Burke/Triolo Productions/Getty Images

Printed in the United States of America
Rodale Inc. makes every effort to use acid-free ♾, recycled paper ♻.

Book design by Joanna Williams

Library of Congress Cataloging-in-Publication Data

Gaines, Edwene.
    The four spiritual laws of prosperity : a simple guide to unlimited abundance /
Edwene Gaines.
        p.   cm.
    ISBN-13 978–1–59486–195–6 hardcover
    ISBN-10 1–59486–195–1 hardcover
    1. Finance, Personal—United States.   2. Spiritual life—United States.   I. Title.
HG179.G256   2005
332.024'01—dc22 2005013081

Distributed to the trade by Holtzbrinck Publishers

6   8   10   9   7   5   hardcover

CONTENTS

I dedicate this work to my bold, beautiful, and brilliant daughter, Maureen, who has taught me to love without conditions.

ACKNOWLEDGMENTS

I am profoundly grateful for the love and wisdom of the many souls who have made enormous contributions to me and this work and encouraged me along the way, including Charles and Myrtle Fillmore, Catherine Ponder, John Rankin, Paula McClellan, Harriet Valliere, John Randolph and Jan Price, Jacob Dean, Joel Dean, Maureen Dempsey, Kenny Smith, Melanie Carson, Kelly Twilley, Barbara Morgan, Kathie Kirby, Joel Fotinos, my collaborator Elsa Hurley, my agent Candice Fuhrman, my editors Stephanie Tade and Jennifer Kushnier, Ed and Angie Gaines, and Corinne Gaines.

INTRODUCTION

My name is Edwene Gaines, and I am a woman of power.

This hasn't always been true. There was a time years ago when my days were filled with fear and deprivation. I had holes in my shoes. I was working two jobs, sixteen hours a day, and still I couldn't make ends meet. Sometimes I didn't even know how I was going to feed my hungry child.

Then I asked God to help me turn my life around. After I did, some of the things I felt called to do seemed a little crazy, but I did them anyway. As a result, my life has been completely transformed. I now own a beautiful retreat center. I travel first class. I have fine clothes, jewelry, and a lovely home. If I want something, I simply buy it. I even have somebody on my staff who buys my toilet paper for me (not that I really minded buying toilet paper, but it's kind of fun that I don't have to do it anymore).

Yes, I am a woman of power, and I am also a woman of passion: It's not enough for me that I now live in comfort and luxury. I have made a commitment that I would be responsible for changing the way that all people think about the potential for prosperity and abundance in their lives. It is my goal that every single person on this planet have faith that all he or she needs and wants in life will appear—and that includes *you*. My mission is not complete until you, too, are living a life of true prosperity. I want to see your life transformed, and my purpose in writing this book is to help you, with a program of practical steps and exercises, to embark on a wondrous new journey—a journey to true prosperity.

So, what is true prosperity? My definition is:

- A vitally alive physical body to provide a comfortable worldly home for the spiritual beings that we are
- Relationships that are satisfying, nurturing, honest, and work all the time
- Work that we love so much that it's not work, it's play
- And all the money we can spend

As a human being living on this planet, your life is subject to a multitude of laws. If you do not obey these laws, things are not going to go the way you want them to go, and you may even find yourself in a whole lot of trouble.

For example, as a physical being, you are governed by the law of physics. Let's say you want to transport a heavy crystal vase from one table to another without breaking it. The law of gravity says that because Earth is pulling on that object, the force you use to carry the vase must be at least as strong, or the vase is going to crash to the floor.

As another example, you are governed by human law, such as that imposed by the State Highway Patrol. Let's say you want to drive your car across the state without getting stopped by the police. You know that if you don't want a speeding ticket, you can't make the trip at 120 miles per hour. You're going to have to obey the speed limit.

Everyone learns about the law of gravity early in life (even if we don't recognize it as such) because, as babies learning to walk, we fell down a lot. And it takes only one experience of seeing those flashing lights in your rearview mirror to know that you need to take human laws seriously. But many people do not know about (and therefore, do not abide by) the spiritual laws that govern their lives, and then they wonder why they can't seem to be rid of credit card debt, get their bills paid, or rise above simply existing from paycheck to paycheck. The reason, of course, is that they are not abiding by the spiritual laws that govern them. And they will not achieve true prosperity until they do.

Here are the four spiritual laws that govern your prosperity:

1. *You must tithe 10 percent of all that you receive to the person, place, or institution where you have received your spiritual food.* Putting God first in your finances is a dynamic act of courage. When you do so, your faith and your ability to stretch yourself, to move forward, and to expand your vision of yourself and your life increases a hundred-fold.

2. *You must set clear-cut, tangible goals.* Goal-setting is looking honestly at where you are, then choosing where you want to be, and then setting a clear and deliberate intention to go there. Doing so forces you to live consciously, rather than unconsciously.

3. *You must forgive everyone all the time, especially yourself.* Forgiveness is a discipline and a powerful spiritual practice that will enable you to feel worthy enough to live prosperously. It requires a diligence and a commitment to compassion and understanding.

4. *You must seek, discover, and follow your divine purpose.* You must assign significance and meaning to your life, giving yourself strength and endurance and bringing joy to your existence on a daily basis. When you are aligned with your divine purpose, you bring a passion to all that you do.

Remember, prosperity is not *just* about money. Do not look at other people and say, "They are not following one of the spiritual laws—such as, say, forgiveness—but they have lots of money. Therefore, the spiritual laws must not really exist." The truth is that you don't know anything about that person's inner life, or how happy his or her relationships are. You cannot accurately judge whether another person is truly prosperous.

The four spiritual laws are just as much a force in your life as is the law of gravity. They are very simple laws, but none of them are optional, and it does not matter a whit if you believe in them or not. They play a powerful role in your life regardless.

Now, you may happen to be a cynic. You may say that you can't just take on faith all of these wild promises I make about what God has in store for you. And that's fine. I'm a cynic myself, by nature. I had to see the results firsthand to believe it, so I understand if you do, too.

Just to prepare you, I'm going to make some claims in this book that may sound hard to believe. I am going to make some statements that may fly in the face of everything you've heard up to this point. All I ask is that you bear with me and give this program a try. Once you see the results, you'll be convinced all on your own. I'm going to ask you to do some things that may feel outrageous to you. You don't have to trust me. You just have to trust God.

Let's say you think something I'm asking you to do sounds a little wacky, or smacks of hocus pocus. Please just keep an open mind, and do it anyway. Ultimately, you don't need me to convince you that what I am saying is true, because the results that will occur in your life will convince you.

> "The question is not 'What if I die tomorrow?' It is, 'What if I live another 20 or 30 years the way I am?'"
>
> —Kim Wolinski

Give yourself six months or so; you have nothing to lose. The system you're using right now isn't working all that brilliantly, is it? You're not so wealthy that you're staggering under the weight of all that abundance, are you? Keep an open mind, act in faith (even when you feel doubt), and simply observe the astonishing changes as they take place in your life. And then prepare yourself, because the kingdom is going to open to you. The only thing is that *you have to give God a chance to make good on God's promises*. And to do that, you have to say, "Maybe this feels like something I wouldn't normally do, but I'm going to try it anyway and see what happens."

Some of my beliefs, as I outline them in this book, may seem very new or unusual to you, and you may wonder how I came to believe them. Well, it's been a long road; my own particular brand of faith did not happen overnight.

I was raised in a fundamentalist faith, and we attended church on a regular basis. As a young child, I enjoyed going to church and believed that we were put here on Earth to be just as good as Jesus was. And yet, every time a preacher spoke, I kept hearing how unworthy, guilty, shameful, polluted, and sinful I was.

As a young child, I took it to heart; I heard the words that I was unworthy and shameful. I was deeply distressed and didn't know what to do about it. I would wrack my brain trying to figure out what these sins were that I had committed, and how I could atone for them. It was terribly painful, but still I continued to attend church up into adolescence and to try to abide by the church's rules. In high school, I didn't even dance because our preacher said it was a sin. I dressed very modestly and was the last girl in my class to start wearing makeup. I really, truly wanted to do the right thing. I had a deep and abiding love for God, but no matter what I did, the message I got was that I just couldn't be good enough.

When I went away to college, I found out that while I'd

been being a good girl, the rest of the world was having a party. So I decided to join in the fun. And the more I got into it, the more I thought, *I can't go back to that church, because I'm not good enough.* Since I'd tried so hard for so long and always come up short, I finally just gave up and said, "To hell with it," and left the church. I still felt a connection with God, but I just didn't know what to do with it, so I put it on the back burner.

My first husband was a Catholic, and I started going to mass with him. I loved the music, the ritual, and the pageantry. I didn't understand a lot (it was pre-Vatican II, so the Masses were in Latin), but I felt the presence of the Virgin Mary, and I loved to talk to her. I went through the conversion process and became a Catholic. I was happy to be a part of the church and was contented to be doing what my husband wanted me to do.

But then, after I had been part of the church for a while, things started going wrong in my life. Really wrong. It turned out I wasn't the only woman who found my husband irresistible, and, being only human, he had yielded to temptation. More than once.

I went to see a priest for help, and what he told me was, in essence, "It's your role in this life to suffer." And I thought, *I don't believe that that is true. I don't believe that suffering was what God had created me to do.*

And so I left the Catholic Church, too.

For many years after, I lived without a church life. Then one day, I met a group of interesting people who all went to a New Thought church in Houston, and I decided to attend once, too, to see what it was all about. And when I started to hear what the people at that church were saying, I couldn't believe my ears.

Some of these things were:

- God is not up on some cloud, distant and unreachable. God is active and present in everything, everywhere, all around us.
- God is within me, and because God is within me, I am naturally good.
- I am not at the mercy of fate. Instead, I create my experiences by what I choose to think and believe.
- I am not alone. Prayer is a tool I can use to connect with God and to receive divine guidance.
- By living my personal truth, I do and give my best to the world. I have the power to make a difference.

I had the overwhelming realization, "These people believe what I believe. This is exactly what I've been looking for!" What a relief! Up to that point I had been told I was less than enough, sinful, and broken. But now I was hearing that I was good, that I was loved, that I was God's child. Instead of all the things about me that I had to fix, suddenly the focus had shifted to all the possibilities in my life.

It took many years, but I eventually was ordained as a minister in the Unity Church (which is one of several churches and organizations that all fall under the umbrella of New Thought). And the work that I do as a minister is joyous and deeply fulfilling. Having said that, however, I would like to be clear that I do not claim—in any way—to be speaking on Unity's behalf in this book. While many of my beliefs originated in the teachings of Unity, my beliefs as I have explained them in this book are the result of many years of prayer, meditation, reading of the Scriptures, and trial and error in my own life. In these pages, I can speak only of what I have chosen to believe, how I have chosen to live, and what I have personally come to understand.

Some of what I outline in this book comes straight from Scripture. Some of it is based on my interpretation of many different prosperity books. Some of it is the philosophy of people I have read and studied, and some of the philosophy is all my own.

If you are Jewish, Buddhist, Muslim, a Hare Krishna, an agnostic, or a member of any other religion, sect, or belief system, you may be wondering whether you can read this book and implement the practices into your life. The answer is that yes, you can. You can benefit from taking the spiritual journey of prosperity without compromising any of your beliefs. The principles of tithing, goal-setting, forgiveness, and finding divine purpose can benefit every single person on this planet, regardless of religion, race, gender, social class, sexual orientation, or any of the many other labels we seem so intent to put on ourselves.

The human Jesus Christ existed; that is widely accepted. Of course, who he was and exactly what role he now plays in our lives has been a matter of discussion for centuries. The Unity Church believes: "Jesus was a special person in history who expressed perfection and thereby became the Christ, or Jesus Christ. He was a Teacher who demonstrated the importance of thoughts, words, and deeds in shaping the life and world of the individual. Jesus' teaching was based on prayer, which to him was conscious communion with God."

Now it may be that your beliefs about Jesus Christ may be very different from that of most Christians, and that is fine. Please do not let your feelings about him prohibit you from reading this book and benefiting from what it has to offer you.

Of course, Jesus is not the only historical figure who embodies for people Godliness and divinity. There is Mohammed, Buddha, the Virgin Mary, Quan Yin, the Dalai Lama, and numerous others. Whatever your beliefs may be, I urge you to deepen your faith in that direction. If, for example, Mohammed is the embodiment of divinity according to your faith and beliefs, by all means ask him to help you in your prosperity journey. Incorporate what you already believe into your new journey, and at the same time let the new ideas you will read here help you deepen the faith that you already have.

There is a line from the play *Inherit the Wind* by Jerome Lawrence and Robert E. Lee where a character is described as having always "looked for God too high up and too far

away." I think that's what so many of us do, in whatever religion or spiritual belief system we might have; we look for
God too high up and too far away.

My belief is that God is right here in this moment,
within us, surrounding us, embracing us, connecting us, and
that the more awake and aware we are to God's presence
within and around us, the more joy, abundance, and vitality
we will be able to experience in our own lives. The mystics
call it "practicing the presence of God." And to me, that is
what life is all about.

Our challenge and our goal is not to try to fight and ma-
nipulate a universe that wants to withhold our good. Instead,
it is to accept that the good is here and to give ourselves permission to receive it. My own experience is that this requires
us to make some very profound and deep-seated changes
within ourselves.

I believe that the presence and power of God is within each
and every human being. We can choose to align with it and to
embrace it, but we can't do that until we adhere to the four
spiritual laws, a process that we will explore in this book.

I believe that prosperity is your birthright, as a child of
God. I believe that it is your divine inheritance, bequeathed
to you by divine right. Prosperity is the consciousness of God
present everywhere. God wants you to be prosperous. And
this book will show you how to be.

I am extremely excited that it is possible for people to
wake up to their inherent divinity. And my excitement and
enthusiasm about the "waking up to divinity" process is that
it works for every single one of us, no matter what we may

have done or chosen to believe in the past. I'm thrilled about the unlimited possibilities that we can unleash from inside ourselves.

Let's conclude with a prayer to launch you on this important journey:

Father/Mother God, I invite the Holy Spirit to take charge of my journey to prosperity. I let go of all that has gone before, and I now begin anew. I am free and forgiven for all the mistakes I've made in the past. I open myself now to expressing a brand new magnificence. I open myself to the infinite possibilities that are mine to choose. I open myself to receiving all the goodness I can have and to all the greatness I can achieve. I invite the Holy Spirit to heal my body, to harmonize my emotions, to renew my mind. To fill me now with a mighty faith that empowers me and allows me to commit to be all that I came to be. Amen.

PART ONE

THE FIRST LAW: TITHING

CHAPTER 1

MASTERING MONEY

We as a human race have managed to build the internal combustion engine, eradicate polio, and make TV dinners you can heat in just minutes in the microwave. But we have not yet learned one of the most important things of all: how to form a healthy attitude toward money. We have to learn to be masters of our money, and not let it be the master of us. We must realize that the power to bring about real and positive change in this world is not in gold bullion, stocks, or bonds. Instead, the power is within *us*, as children of God, at the level of our spirituality.

Money is a means to an end, not the end itself. You cannot eat money, and it cannot keep you warm or cuddle you at night. Simply having money is not the goal. The goal is to use it to do whatever your heart leads you to do, and to do that which fulfills your divine purpose.

Many people who attend my workshops struggle with conflicting issues of morality and money. Perhaps you do, too. Perhaps you've been brought up to believe that money is evil. Perhaps you were taught the myth of noble poverty—that good people don't dream about wealth and prosperity, because doing so is greedy. As a result, part of you chooses to remain poor, and your life feels constrained and unfulfilled. You may have a sense that your dreams will never be achieved, and you live with the fear that life is passing you by.

Then perhaps another part of you—the part that caused you to pick up this book—believes that God wants more for you, that it's not God's will for you to endlessly struggle from paycheck to paycheck. In your heart you know that God loves you and wants the best for you. You sense that God has a special plan for you, and that if only you had the financial means, you could be out in the world, doing God's work and making a positive difference in the lives of other people, as well as fully making the most of this precious life that God has blessed you with.

A lot of us are torn between these two sides of ourselves because of the contradictory messages we've gotten our whole lives concerning spirituality and money. It's no wonder that when it comes to our finances, so many people feel conflicted and confused.

LEARNING TO ACCEPT OUR DESIRES

Many people want something—a house, a car, a new pair of shoes—but feel that they can't afford it. So they feel virtuous when they let themselves off the hook by saying, "Oh, I don't really want that thing. And anyway, I shouldn't be so materialistic."

Contrary to popular belief, God doesn't love a martyr. I

should know; I played one for many years. Denying our material desires is not what God wants us to do. What we could choose to do instead is grow, develop our courage and faith, and stand up and say without guilt or hesitation, "This is what I want!"

If you desire something, and then you deny that you desire it, that's cowardice and spiritual laziness. And what's more, it's a lie.

God wants us to do more, to have more, to play big. God doesn't want us to deny our desires. After all, God put those desires in us, and we must celebrate them! Life is not about struggling, and being unhappy, and then dying. It is about enjoying and appreciating everything life has to offer. Through joy, we glorify God.

These ideas may be new to you. They often are to the people who attend my seminars, and those people often have lots of questions. Let me pose some of the most common questions and share my ideas about them.

"WHAT IS MONEY, ANYWAY?"

There is a lot written about what money is. Some scholars say it is "deferred service." Some say it is energy. Some believe that money is a spiritual symbol of invisible spiritual substance. Spiritual substance is what the mystics call the invisible body of God out of which all things are created—your clothes, your jewelry, your shoes, and the chair you are sitting in. It's all created out of one invisible substance called the body of God.

Money is an energy system we are using right now, which I believe will one day disappear. Money will no longer be necessary. Because, as Charles Fillmore, the cofounder of the Unity Church, says, "We shall serve for the joy of serving." And when we do, everything that we need and want will flow to us. So we won't need money.

But money is not going to disappear until we have mastered it, until we know that there is really no power in it, that it's here as an item to serve us, and that we don't have to earn it, or struggle for it, or do anything we don't want to do to get money. We certainly don't have to work a job we hate for it.

I believe that God is not way high up, way far away. I believe God is within us. I believe God is a part of everything we see and do, no matter how mundane. And what is more mundane than money? We touch it and handle it every day, in so many big and small different ways. You carry it with you. Every single piece of our money, down to the lowly penny, has a prayer on it: *In God we trust.*

"IS IT GREEDY TO DESIRE MATERIAL GOODS?"

Being rich doesn't mean you're greedy or bad. Still, when we think of accumulating wealth, many of us think of Ebenezer Scrooge, counting his coins in a cold, unlit room, and we don't want to be like that. We may instinctively dislike and distrust people when we feel that they want everything for themselves, and nothing for anyone else.

But this need not be the case. Let's take as an example Oprah Winfrey, who has far, far more money than any one person could ever need or possibly spend. If great wealth is an indicator of greed, then she must be one of the greediest people on the planet. But do we think that Oprah is greedy and materialistic because she lives in lavish mansions? Of course not! We're too busy paying rapt attention to how she went to South Africa to work with AIDS orphans. We admire her for her genuine care for other people and for her giving and generous spirit.

Greed is when you say, "I want this, and I don't want you to have it." It's not greedy to say, "I want lots, and I want you to have lots, too." If you believe that there is no end to God's abundance, then everyone should have all that they want, and then more.

Money is like love: The more you give away, the more you have. Love is a limitless resource, and so is money, and both were created by God to enrich our lives and allow us to live fully, joyfully, and completely. And you're going to discover the truth of the law of compensation, that you cannot outgive God. Emerson said that: *You cannot outgive God.* And he was absolutely correct.

"WHAT ABOUT THE SCRIPTURAL PASSAGES THAT PREACH AGAINST MATERIALISM?"

I get this question a lot, especially regarding the passage from the Book of Mark that states that it is easier for a camel to pass through the eye of the needle than it is for a rich man to enter the gates of heaven.

There are a lot of different interpretations of this Scripture. One is that there was an entry gate into Jerusalem called "The Eye of the Needle" because it was so small. Camels that came along with large cargo had to be unloaded so that the camel could get through and then be reloaded on the other side. If this is the eye of the needle the Scripture is referring to—and we do not know this conclusively—then it is merely more difficult (but not impossible) for a richly loaded camel to pass through.

I believe that sometimes you have to be willing to give up the good to receive the greater good. At some point, as we gain more and more, we realize our material possessions are not that which is truly making us happy, and we can move beyond them to another spiritual level. At that point, we unload our camels and proceed without the cargo. When we do, we are the master of the material goods, not the other way around. We do not *need* our material things, and we reach a place of happily letting go. You have made spiritual progress when you can have your things or not, and be happy regardless.

> "If we would only give, just once, the same amount of reflection to what we want to get out of life that we give to the question of what to do with a two-week vacation, we would be startled at our false standards and the aimless procession of our busy days."
>
> —Dorothy Canfield Fisher

I think it's interesting that there are so very many scriptural references to prosperity and yet people tend to latch on to the ones that seem to suggest the nobility of poverty. But the Bible is full of promises of prosperity and abundance—far more than admonitions that suggest the virtue of doing without.

The danger of money comes when we forget what it's there for. When it begins to cloud the parts of our lives that are much more important, such as the personal relationships we have with the people we love, or our personal relationship with God.

That's what happened to me when, at one point in my life, I married a very wealthy man. I forgot some basic truths. I forgot that money is valuable in what it can allow us to do, be, and enjoy, and instead mistook money as being valuable in and of itself.

I had come into great prosperity, but I forgot why I was on this planet. I got so wrapped up in the money and the beautiful material things I owned that I let go of the spiritual world and kind of drowned in all the luxury. My life became stale and stagnant.

Over time, the riches caused me to depart from my spiritual pathway. I lost my appreciation for the small things. And at some point the lavish house in the posh district of town came to feel like a prison. The wealth became a burden.

There is a story in the Bible of a rich young ruler who went to Jesus and asked, "What must I do to have eternal life?" and Jesus said, "Sell everything you own, give the money to the poor, and come follow me."

I finally had to admit to myself that perhaps I had entered the marriage for the wrong reasons, and the relationship ended. I left that expensive house full of beautiful furniture, leaving everything behind except the clothes on my back and some things I could put in my car. As I drove away, I felt like the rich young ruler in that I had to leave behind all my worldly goods. That was what I needed in that moment because it forced me to get back to my true nature and calling.

The mistake I think people make, however, is that they think they should *always* be forfeiting their material goods.

But I don't believe that I—or you, or anyone—need to live a lifetime of desperation or poverty. In that moment, however, it was what I needed as a wake-up call and to keep my life from going any farther down the wrong track, away from my sense of spirituality, and what I knew to be true and important.

Once again, the issue is whether you are the master of your money, or if your money and worldly objects are the master of you. There are times in your life when you are using money as a tool to do the work you need to do on this Earth. At other times in your life, you might start getting mesmerized by the glitter of the gold, and momentarily forget what's really important to you. At those times, your money is mastering you.

"ISN'T POVERTY A VIRTUE?"

People tend to think this. But, I ask, if poverty is so great, why is a fundamental goal of the major religions to eradicate it?

I was raised in a fundamentalist faith, and I have read and reread the Bible all my life. And nowhere did I read, "Thou shalt learn to do without, to be and have less than you could, to be less than God sent you to be." Instead it says, "It is your Father's good pleasure to give you the kingdom," and by "kingdom," I believe Jesus meant not just the kingdom of heaven but also the joy of a life richly led right here on Earth.

During a period of terrible poverty, I went and got a red letter Bible (a Bible in which everything Jesus said was printed in red). Everything Jesus said was so positive. He urged us to ask for what we want, and to not be afraid. The stories he told were success stories, about people triumphing over incredible odds, and my thought was, *I believe my loving God wants more for me in life than just a miserable existence where I don't know how I'm going to put food on the table.*

Nobody wants to live in poverty. I've been there, and it's a terrible place to be. It's awful to wonder how you're going to pay the light bill or to suspect that someone might be coming to repossess your car. There's just nothing fun about it, and God wants us to have fun.

How do you live the life you're meant to live? You live real close to God. You acknowledge that you are a child of God, you're made in the image and likeness of the Most High, you're a spiritual being, and it is the Father's good pleasure to give you the kingdom.

You are rich with unlimited possibility. If you don't believe that, then you are spiritually poor, and will be living in constant physical poverty. Only when you genuinely believe that you are blessed with unlimited possibility can prosperity come into your life.

"WASN'T JESUS POOR?"

This is simply not true; he did not live a life of poverty. Jesus did not carry money with him, but everything he needed was provided for him in abundance. He stayed in good homes and ate the best food.

According to Scripture, Jesus had a seamless garment. Just think of the clothes you are wearing today and how many seams they have. Can you imagine the hours of labor that must go into making a seamless garment, and what it must have been worth? At the crucifixion, the centurions cast lots to see who would get that seamless garment.

"ARE WE DRAINING OUR NATURAL RESOURCES BY CONSUMING SO MUCH?"

Some people don't ask for what they want because they feel the world's supply is limited, and there isn't enough to go around. But this belief is false. "Well, what about the people starving in Ethiopia?" you might ask. I would answer that every day in this world, enough fruit falls off the trees and rots on the ground that could feed the globe. There is enough. We have a problem of distribution. We have not yet made it a priority to get the fruit to the hungry people before the fruit goes bad. But in terms of quantity, there is more than enough.

The truth is that we live in a lavish and abundant universe, in which everything we could ever want or need can and will be provided to us. And if we don't lay hold of what God provides, that's not God's fault. It's ours.

WE MUST LEARN TO ASK

There is a scriptural quote that I love so much, I sometimes have it printed on my stationery: "And whatsoever ye shall ask in my name, that will I do, that the Father may be glorified in the Son." (John 14:13)

Isn't that wonderful? It says, in essence, "Whatever it is that you want, if you ask for it in my name, you'll get it." The promise is so straightforward, and there are no qualifiers. No if's, and's or but's. There's no, "As long as it's a good idea . . ." or "Just so long as it doesn't seem greedy . . ." It doesn't say any of that. It says, "Whatsoever ye shall ask in my name, that I will do . . ." In the name of this indwelling Christ, this indwelling Christ will do for you so that you can glorify God.

Let me tell you something. God is not glorified by poverty. God is not glorified by illness. God is not glorified when you feel guilty or unworthy. God is not glorified when you run around playing the victim.

> "The curious paradox is that when I accept myself just as I am, then I can change."
>
> —Carl Rogers

God *is* glorified when you stand up and acknowledge who you are and claim your birthright. And who are you? You are a divine being, a child of God the Most High, a person who deserves to have every good thing that life has to offer.

Now, it may be that some of the things I'm telling you here are hard for you to accept. They might be the opposite of what you've been told all your life, and you might feel that you can't just transform your thinking instantly, as if by magic. Learning a brand new way of thinking can take some time and concerted effort, so I'd like to introduce a practice that many people find helpful in changing a long-held mindset: affirmations.

An affirmation is a statement about what is *really* true (despite what outward appearances may lead one to believe). When you make a positive statement with conviction, you open up a space in your life for that good to appear.

I suggest you try using affirmations to launch you on your new journey. Write them out, and then speak them aloud three times a day for 21 days. And as you're speaking the words, don't mumble! Speak them with power, from your solar plexus. Say the affirmation as if you absolutely believe it, without a trace of doubt.

Below are some affirmations that I like. You may feel free to use them, or you may want to make up some of your own. If you make up some of your own, remember the key is that you are making a statement about what you desire *as if it is already true.*

You might say any or all of the following:

- My Father/Mother God loves me.
- I am God's beloved child.
- I am forgiven for all mistakes of the past.
- It is God's good pleasure to give me the kingdom.
- I seek the kingdom in all that I experience.
- Because I serve God, I have a right to the abundant life. I have a right to riches.
- Every one of God's children has a right to abundance.
- Because I give of my time, energy, and money, I am in the flow of inexhaustible substance.
- I love to tithe to where I receive my spiritual food. I give lavishly and joyously.
- Rich, divine ideas flow through me to bless and prosper all humankind. I want God's good for everyone.
- My abundance benefits everyone, and everyone's abundance benefits me.
- I set specific goals and let God lead me to accomplish them.
- I am thankful for all my seen and unseen blessings.

- My faith in God is firmly established. I live by faith.
- My thoughts, words, and deeds are divinely creative.
- Because I am faithful in small matters, my Lord makes me master over great matters.
- Never do I seek personal credit; I glorify God in all that I do.
- I am a world server. I serve God in the world. I walk through the world transforming it as I go.
- I am joyous, peaceful, healthy, enthusiastic, wise, loving, and rich. Praise God!
- Forgiveness is my daily business. And I am faithful in prayer to cleanse my emotional nature of bitterness, irritation, blame, and guilt.
- God and I are in the business of loving, giving, and serving.
- I serve God.
- Money serves me.

The truth is that you can have everything you want in this life. You can be free from the grips of poverty, and instead live a life of joy and faith and prosperity. You can live according to your divine purpose, in line with God's plan, with everything you could possibly want or need at your fingertips. If only you can learn to master money.

Mastering money while moving into prosperity is what you will learn to do through the simple but vital principles laid out in this book. And it is a journey that I promise will change your life.

So let's get started.

CHAPTER 2

WHAT IS TITHING?

To start you on your journey toward prosperity, I'd like to first introduce you to the ancient spiritual law of tithing. Tithing means giving back to God one-tenth of everything you receive. And why shouldn't you? After all, you commonly say "Thank you" and give a gift of appreciation to someone who has been very generous with you. Why not with God?

Simply stated, tithing will change your life. When I think of a metaphor for the results of tithing, I think of windows opening and a shower of sparkling gold coming in. But even though tithing produces remarkable results in people's lives, that doesn't mean the practice comes easily or naturally to everyone who hears about it. In fact, tithing is the prosperity principle that tends to bring up the most resistance in people. And I have come to understand that any resistance people feel toward tithing invariably comes from a fear that there will not be enough to go around. But the truth is that we live in a lavish and abundant world, where all our wants and needs will always be provided for—something you will come to learn firsthand on your journey to prosperity.

But I do understand folks' anxieties about tithing. In my own life, tithing hasn't always come easily for me. In fact, it once was a difficult and frightening concept that I had to wrestle with for a long time before I was finally willing to give it a try.

PENNILESS AND DESPERATE

I first began to seek God in an intentional and conscious way about thirty years ago. I was a single parent, working two demanding jobs, living with my daughter in a one-bedroom apartment, and sleepwalking through what Thoreau called a life of "quiet desperation."

My daughter and I were in a continual financial crisis. We often didn't have enough food to eat and survived on peanut butter and crackers for weeks at a time. We both had holes in our shoes. She was embarrassed about taking lunch money to school in pennies, which I managed to find between the cushions of the couch or at the bottom of my purse. One Christmas, we bought ourselves a tiny 39-cent ivy plant as our only Christmas present.

It's not that I was lazy—on the contrary. I was working very hard, many hours, but still we never had enough. There was always another doctor bill or dental bill or car repair or something that stopped me from getting ahead. My frustration was immense.

When it comes to money, I am a person of integrity. If I owe you money, I will pay you back before I will buy food. But in those days, the money simply was not there, and I couldn't pay my bills. This mortified me, but I couldn't work more than two jobs and still be a mother to my child.

One day, I was sitting on the floor in tears, holding my checkbook, surrounded by the bills that I couldn't pay. I became completely overwhelmed with despair. Deep in the throes of self-pity, I raged out in an irreverent, screaming prayer—for answers, for help, for relief, for some glimmer of response from what felt like an unfeeling, uncaring universe.

From my aching and passionate longing, I screamed out, "Now see here, God! I believe that Jesus meant it when he said, 'I have come that you might have life, and live it abundantly.' I don't think he lied to us, but I obviously am not living abundantly. Show me how!"

At the time, I was not involved with any church or religious organization. I had no prayer life and no discipline in spiritual practices. However, I still had a respect for the Bible from my childhood. And when I cried out to God, I felt a clear urge to go find my dusty old King James Bible, which I had not looked at in years. When I picked it up, it fell open to the book of Malachi, Chapter 3, Verse 10: "Bring ye all the tithes into the storehouse, that there may be meat in mine house, and prove me now herewith, saith the Lord of hosts, if I will not open you the windows of heaven, and pour you out a blessing, that there shall not be room enough to receive it."

The New Living Bible puts it this way: "Bring all the tithes into the storehouse so there will be enough food in my Temple. If you do, says the Lord Almighty, I will open the windows of heaven for you. I will pour out a blessing so great that you won't have enough room to take it in! Try it! Let me prove it to you! Your crops will be abundant, for I will guard them from insects and disease. Your grapes will not shrivel before they are ripe, says the Lord Almighty. Then all nations will call you blessed for your Land will be such a delight . . ." (Malachi 3:10–12)

I must have read that Scripture a hundred times that day. I was terrified, looking for a loophole, trying to convince myself that it couldn't mean *me*. I couldn't afford to tithe! I couldn't even afford to properly care for my daughter. How could I give away 10 percent of my money? There was no way I could be so irresponsible. The whole idea of me giving away the little money we had was outrageous.

DOUBTING THOMAS, DOUBTING EDWENE

Tithing wasn't a new concept for me, not by a long shot. In fact, I had heard about tithing all my life in the Baptist church. Every Sunday our preacher got up in his pulpit and talked to the congregation about the importance of tithing. But I suspected it was just a trick to get our money. And he wasn't going to get his hands on *my* money, because I was smarter than he was. Besides, I believed that God didn't need my money, anyway.

And I'd heard about tithing since then, from other people. For example, by the time my daughter and I were getting into bad financial straits I had started seeking answers by reading Catherine Ponder and Charles Fillmore's prosperity books, which discussed tithing. But when I came to a chapter on tithing, I would skip it and go on to the next one. I did all the other things the authors told me to, such as saying affirmations and making a treasure map. (A treasure map is a concrete object—sometimes called a pictured prayer—that is, perhaps, a collage of images and pictures that you can make to help you focus on and attain your goals.) Despite my concerted efforts, however, nothing happened in my life that made me feel that I was moving any closer to prosperity.

One day I went to see a minister I knew. I told him, "John, this prosperity stuff is a nice little airy fairy philosophy, but it doesn't work."

"Do you tithe?" he asked.

"No, I don't," I said. "Why do all of you preachers always harp on about the same things?"

Luckily John was someone who loved me enough to allow me to be angry with him. "Edwene," he said with a sigh, "I am very busy. I have a lot of people waiting to see me who are willing to practice spiritual law. You obviously are not. Please excuse me." And to my indignation and annoyance, he escorted me right back out of his office.

The truth is that I am a cynic, as I've told you. My training is in journalism. It's my job to question, to doubt, to demand solid proof. That's why I've always been glad there was a Doubting Thomas in the New Testament. Doubting Thomas had to actually stick his hands into Jesus' wounds to make sure that was the very same Jesus that was up there on the cross. He couldn't just accept it on faith. And when it came to the concept of tithing, and of what it could bring into my life, neither could I.

However, it was one thing to try to tune out the voice of a minister, but it was another to try to tune out the voice of God. By the time I prayed for help and was sent the passage on tithing out of the Bible, even I had to stop and think that maybe this was a concept I should consider more carefully. A little voice inside me said, "Edwene? What if there really is something to this tithing law? What if it really can lead to riches and prosperity? And what if, because of your fear and your self-righteousness and your cynical attitude and the fact you think you know it all, you miss out?" Well, that little voice got my attention because I didn't want to miss out on riches and prosperity.

I looked again at the passage from Malachi: "Bring ye all the tithes into the storehouse, that there may be meat in mine house, and prove me now herewith, saith the Lord of hosts, if I will not open you the windows of heaven and pour you out a blessing, that there shall not be room enough to receive it." And three words jumped out at me: "Prove me now."

> "We do not see things as they are. We see them as we are."
>
> —The *Talmud*

I realized that in this passage, God was offering a great and generous gift of proving this to us. I think this must be the *only* place in the Bible where God gives us this opportunity. After all, the Bible doesn't attempt to prove God. It doesn't start out arguing and explaining why you should believe that God exists. Instead, it assumes that you will believe. It simply starts out, "In the beginning God created the heavens and the Earth." You are supposed to accept that fact completely, without argument. And certainly without a chance to put God to a true test. But Malachi 3:10 says that we can prove God.

Try it! says the Scripture. *Let me prove it to you!*

Finally, I did.

I realized that I was being offered a choice. That choice was to believe God's promise—or not. All belief is choice. We have the power to choose what we believe. All the same, I wish I could say that I began to tithe with a lot of faith, but I didn't. I began to tithe with just the small amount of faith necessary to begin. I know now that is the Truth for all things. All we need is enough to begin. Then we learn to trust more. The more we choose to believe a spiritual promise and then see that the promise is kept, the more we have faith.

My conversation with God that first day went something like this: "Okay, Pops, I'm terrified. But this Scripture seems like an answer to prayer, so I'm going to tithe—but only for six months. That's all you've got—six months to prove yourself in my life. And let me tell you, Big Fella, the windows of heaven better open wide!"

GIVING GOD A CHANCE

So I began. I wanted so much to believe that there was a God who would respond to me, but I didn't know for sure that there was. I was filled with anxiety and fear. I didn't tell anyone what I was doing because I felt a little crazy.

I started to tithe with a faith the size of a mustard seed. I promised myself that for six months, I would give 10 percent of any income to the person, place, or institution from which I received my spiritual food. Spiritual food, I believe, is that which inspires us and causes us to remember who and what we are—children of the living God, with infinite possibilities for expression and with no end of joy in our lives.

I got myself a little notebook and wrote down every penny that came in—salary, bonus, garage sale money, everything. If I found a dime on the sidewalk, I wrote it down and tithed on it to acknowledge God as my source.

I'd like to tell you that when I first started making tithes I did so with faith, freely and cheerfully, but the truth was I was scared silly. I tithed with absolute terror. Some days I gave away money knowing that I'd have none left for me and my daughter to buy groceries and eat the next day, and yet I gave it away regardless. But I had said that I was going to give God a chance to make good on this promise, and I had made a commitment that I intended to keep.

In those first fearful months, I learned a great deal. In the dead of night I sometimes experienced panic attacks and night terrors. It was very scary. I did a lot of affirmations, such as, "Creditors can't eat me. Creditors can't eat me!" I learned how important it was to turn back to prayer, to re-read some faith-building literature, to listen to an inspirational tape, to write out statements of faith to remind myself what I had chosen to believe. And yet, no matter how scared I got, I never stopped tithing. My rationale was that if this promise of tithing was not going to be true for me, I'd rather know it now than later.

When any money came in, such as a paycheck, I would tithe on it before I did anything else. Before I paid any bills, I would take 10 percent of the paycheck and send it to a place or person that had recently given me spiritual food.

And then, as my bills would come in (for which I now didn't have enough money), I would write out the check, bless it, put it in the envelope, put a stamp on it, ready to mail. I would tell God, "I'm ready. I don't have the money yet, but I'm ready to mail this when the money shows up."

For the first few weeks, nothing much happened. My dreams of heaven's windows being thrown open were not realized. But although my greatest dreams weren't realized, neither were my worst fears. The electric company did not turn off my service. Nor did anyone come to repossess my car. Somehow, there was food on the table at every meal. My daughter and I did not starve.

And then, once I had been tithing for a while, some very interesting things started to happen. Out of the blue, I'd get a refund check from somebody. Or I'd get a little $5 gift from Aunt Mary, or my Dad would give me $20. Money would start coming in little dribs and drabs. By the end of three months, my income was doubled. As a schoolteacher on a tiny income, that got my attention.

Part of why it was so hard for me to start tithing at all in the first place was that I was very hard-headed and self-reliant, the kind of person who, when offered help or charity, would say, "I can take care of myself, thank you very much!" So, I had to learn to trust God, to become like a little child and let someone else take charge. I had to give up completely. It was a powerful lesson in learning humility, in accepting the angels that God sent to me. When a friend offered a cash gift, I couldn't let pride stand in the way. I had to learn to accept these kindnesses with grace and gratitude.

As I continued to tithe over a few months, my faith grew, and so did my determination and vision. New ideas occurred to me. I began to realize that all those businesses I saw around the town square were operating by faith and that I, too, had some talent and skills that I could use. For example, I saw that in my little community no one was doing advertising and public relations work. I wondered if perhaps that was a void I could fill. After all, I had a degree in journalism and could write and take photographs. Wonderful synchronistic events began to occur. As I continued to step out in faith and act on the divine ideas that flowed to me, my confidence and joy expanded.

A WEALTHY FATHER

At one point, as tithing was proving to be a positive force in my life and was becoming a regular habit of mine, I decided to go into business for myself. At that point I was still working two jobs, sometimes sixteen hours a day. One of my jobs had a very fancy title and a tiny salary to go with it: I was the Coordinator of Community Relations for the Conroe, Texas, Independent School District. It was very prestigious; I mean, I was "Miss It," or as we say in Alabama, "Miss Thang." But I wasn't making any money.

I decided that the only way I was going to get ahead was to take a leap of faith. I had to quit the job and open up a business. Since I didn't know how to run a business, I had to trust that God was going to be willing to go into business with me. Otherwise, I didn't stand a chance.

So, I went to my boss, the school superintendent, and I said, "I want to resign and go into business for myself."

"Edwene, you can't do that," he told me. "The economy is so bad right now. If you go into business and it doesn't work out, you're going to lose everything. And you have a child to support!"

He didn't know the worst of it: that I didn't know how to run a business! I knew that I could never ever explain to him what I was doing. I couldn't tell him, "Not only am I going to quit, but I have started tithing, which means I am freely giving away a good chunk of all my money." The poor man would have had a heart attack.

So instead I said, "Thank you for your concern. I really appreciate it. But what you don't understand is that I have a father who is really, really rich, so I don't have to worry. If anything happens, he'll take care of me."

> "A step in the wrong direction is better than staying on the spot all our life. Once you're moving forward you can correct your course as you go. Your automatic guidance system cannot guide you when you're standing still."
>
> —Maxwell Maltz

I didn't want the superintendent to worry about me or feel that he was in some way responsible for my welfare.

Of course, the father I was talking about was God.

"Oh," my boss said. "Great. Well, in that case, go right ahead. And good luck to you."

And so I did. I went out and started a new business. And I took some big risks, too. In Texas, when you resign from the school system, you may take your money out of the Teacher Retirement System. If you later change your mind and want to come back, you have to put it all back in, or you can't start teaching again. Well, the first thing I did after

I quit was to take all of my money out of Teacher Retirement and spend it (after tithing on it, of course). It felt like a risky thing to do, but I didn't want to have that money to fall back on in case I failed. I didn't want a safety net. Either God was going to be my net, or God wasn't, and I wanted to know the truth sooner rather than later. Wouldn't you?

Unity cofounder Charles Fillmore says in his book *Prosperity* that when we begin to tithe, our faith increases a hundred-fold, and this was true for me. Although I was in the midst of poverty, my new faith enabled me to act on the divine ideas that came to me. With no financial backing, no investors, and very little money, I went into business with God. And we were very successful.

THE WINDOWS OF HEAVEN OPENED, FINALLY

I gave God a chance to prove the tithing promise to me, and God did so beyond my wildest imaginings. I opened not one but two highly profitable companies, making them up as I went along, asking for guidance for even the simplest things. I had the PR business, and I ran a personal success center where I counseled others who needed spiritual guidance and success coaching.

My daughter, who was eleven at the time, licked stamps, sorted papers, made lists, and did other odd jobs. We laughed and cried and kept breaking through the limiting boundaries we had created around our lives.

By the end of three months, my income had doubled. At

the end of six, it had tripled. As money came in from my new businesses, I lost my fear of not having food for my child. As profits rose, I was able to buy new clothing for her and myself and some other necessities we had done without. Soon, there was even some extra money just for having fun. At that point, though I had come to the end of my contract with God, I wasn't about to stop. Even though I still had moments of doubt, tithing had become a way of life for me, and I kept going.

At the end of the first year of tithing, I had received more than $100,000.

I married a very successful man, and life during our marriage was affluent. I had a beautiful new home in the best part of town. I was given a brand-new Cadillac and an expensive diamond ring. I could go to dinner at an upscale gourmet restaurant as easily as I could go to McDonald's. (This chapter of my life, as I've already shared with you, had its own ups and downs.)

> "All changes, even the most longed for, have their melancholy; for what we leave behind is part of ourselves; we must die to one life before we can enter into another."
>
> —Anatole France

In the years since, I have continued to push through my fears and refused to waver in my commitment to tithe. Placing my wholehearted faith in the invisible substance of God has empowered me to experience the presence of divinity in my everyday life. And it has enabled me to empower others along the way.

I love to share what I have learned about tithing, and to

watch it work its magic in the lives of others. One such person, a woman named Jill, has graciously allowed me to share her story.

JILL'S STORY OF TITHING

At 28 years old, Jill had hit the lowest point in her life. She was four years into a bankruptcy, had little-to-no marketable skills, and had the feeling that she was not just floundering, but actually going under. Her life wasn't working on any front. She was virtually penniless, had very few friends, and her head was full of negative, venomous self-talk. Selling real estate part-time, which Jill had done in the past, was no longer working or generating any badly needed money. Finally, unable to pay rent, Jill was evicted from her apartment and forced to move into an abandoned trailer with no heat, electricity, or water.

It was then that Jill realized she had come to a crossroads in her life. She had to either completely reinvent her life, or end it. In despair, feeling helpless and hopeless, she started planning to end it. She gave herself thirty days to make the final decision one way or the other.

It was during this thirty-day period that Jill first attended one of my seminars. She later told me that the seminar planted a seed of hope in her heart—the first feeling of hope she had felt in years. She made a commitment to herself to try tithing, and to do forgiveness work. She began writing her goals and posting them around her trailer. It took only four months of tithing for her financial life to turn around.

She found a job. Once again she was earning a good wage, and she was able to look for new housing.

Jill was doing so well, in fact, that she decided she no longer needed to tithe, and stopped. Within two months, her life had fallen apart again. So she started to tithe again and was able to pick up the pieces. Jill would repeat this pattern—tithing and then stopping—over the next year and a half until she finally saw it clearly. When she tithed, life was prosperous and harmonious. When she stopped tithing, her life fell apart. She would have a fight with her boss, or a car accident, or an illness that required doctor visits (which were expensive because she had no insurance). After about eighteen months of fighting the law of tithing, Jill finally "got it." Tithing worked, in a big and real way. Jill understood that, for her, tithing was not an option, but a necessity.

> "Journeys bring power and love back into you. If you can't go some-where, move in the passageways of the self. They are like shafts of light, always changing, and you change when you explore them."
>
> —Rumi

During this time Jill also found a few self-development seminars that helped her incorporate forgiveness, concrete goal setting, and finding her divine purpose into her daily life. Her life continued to change for the better. Within two years, she was gainfully employed, had moved out of the trailer into a nice house, had lots of new friends, and was finally free of the crippling sense of hopelessness that had once led her to seriously consider ending her life.

Now, fifteen years later, Jill is a millionaire. She has a large, diverse investment portfolio and a beautiful home with a steam sauna; she travels the world as often as she likes and has recorded two CDs. Perhaps more to the point, she is also extremely happy. She is living the life she always dreamed, serving the world with her music and her financial coaching.

Jill not only continues to tithe, but she now pre-tithes—tithing in advance to receiving money, knowing always that we "cannot outgive God." She meets regularly with a mastermind team of accountability partners who keep her on track with her goals. She also continues to incorporate forgiveness into her daily prayers and practices.

Jill states that she would not be alive today if she hadn't learned about tithing, forgiveness, and goal-setting. She says, "They produce actual results that can be taken to the bank and deposited, both financially and spiritually. If your life isn't going the way you hoped, you must give these spiritual practices a chance. They will change your life."

The Law of Tithing generates more questions among the people I share it with than any other prosperity principle. In the following pages, I answer some of the most frequently asked questions about tithing. Please understand that these are the answers that I present today, and that I give myself permission to change and grow. For now, however, these answers serve me well.

TITHING QUESTIONS
AND ANSWERS

What is a tithe?

The word "tithe" means a tenth. To tithe is to return 10 percent of all we receive to a person, place, or institution from which we have received spiritual food.

What is spiritual food?

Spiritual food is that which inspires us, teaches us, reminds us of the Truth, and causes us to remember who we really are. It is the infilling of spiritual energy that reconnects us consciously to the awareness of our own innate divinity.

I believe that many people walk around with a hunger—a hunger for a deeper spiritual faith and for a great realization of mission, purpose, and identity. The spiritual food that can feed this hunger can come in many forms. For example, it might be the uplifting message of an inspirational book or the feeling of joy from a beautiful piece of music. Whatever the form, you know you're being spiritually fed when you feel your heart sing.

What is the purpose of the tithe?

The purpose of the tithe is not to build churches or to pay ministers' salaries, although tithes do help to do these and other good things. The real purpose of the tithe is to acknowledge that God is the source of our good and that we are aware and grateful for the good in our lives.

What is the tithing promise?

If we tithe, we prove God in our lives, and the windows of heaven open for us.

God doesn't need my money. Why should I tithe?

Of course God doesn't need your money. You need to give because tithing is a beginning discipline in giving and receiving. It increases our faith and pushes us through conscious fear. When we tithe, we give back to the universe, and when the universe gives back to us, and more, we learn that we cannot outgive God.

Why 10 percent?

The first recorded tithe in the Bible is discussed in Genesis 14, when Abraham took his tithe to his spiritual teacher, Melchizedek. We are not told why 10 percent, only that it is 10 percent.

Personally, I think God made the tithe 10 percent—and not, say, 11.3 percent—because God knew that some of us were not going to be very good at mathematics. Can you imagine the math required to tithe 11.3 percent?

What if I receive spiritual food from several places?

Most of us do. It seems perfectly logical to split our tithe and send a portion of it to all those persons, places, and institutions that have fed us spiritual food.

What if those I tithe to don't need it?

Our tithes must go to those who have fed us spiritual food. We must not consider whether the recipients are rich or poor—that is not our concern. Our concern is to acknowledge God as our source by giving 10 percent to those who feed us spiritual food.

Do we tithe net or gross?

The answer is found in the question, "Do you want to prosper a little or a lot?" My suggestion is to tithe on gross. My belief is that the more you give, the more you surrender in faith to God, the more you receive. When you tithe gross, you're telling God you're serious in your commitment to prosperity. When I tithe gross I can almost imagine God saying, "Whoo-ey! I got me a player here!"

I believe that when we question the finer points of tithing, what we are really asking is, "How little can I get by with giving and still be okay?" Rather than ask that question, it's better to develop faith that you will always be okay, because God will take care of you.

And in fact, some people choose to tithe *more* than gross. For example, Dr. Tom Costa is a Religious Science minister in Palm Desert, California. He and I were on a speakers program one year in Canada. One day, he told me his tithing story.

"Last year I decided that instead of tithing one-tenth of what I received, I would tithe one-tenth of what I *wanted* to receive. I started on January first. And at the end of the year my CPA and I looked at the numbers, and my income had caught up to the level of my tithing." Then, after telling me this story, Tom took me outside to show me his new Rolls Royce.

What do you do about the money that you made before you started tithing?

Start where you are now. Before you're through, you're going to give it all to God, anyway. But don't worry about the past. Start with your 10 percent now.

What if my partner (spouse/family) doesn't believe in tithing?

We are responsible for obeying spiritual laws as we understand them. It is appropriate to share with your partner your commitment to acknowledge God as the source of your good, and then ask your partner what portion of the income is yours to tithe on. This could possibly upset some apple carts, but they would be apple carts that needed to be upset. Any sort of relationship that works must be based on the equality of the participants. Besides, when they see the results of tithing in our lives, they will probably want to tithe, too.

When do I tithe?

The sooner we tithe on income received, the sooner we make room for more to flow in. You may choose to write your tithe checks and send them out immediately after receiving income. If you have a regular place of worship, you may take your tithe to the ministry class or worship service. There is one of two things going on in this universe at all times: There is circulation, or there is congestion. If we hold on to our tithe, what we are saying to the universe is, "Don't send me any more. I haven't tithed on this yet."

What do I tithe on?

We tithe on all money that we receive. Salary, bonuses, interest earned, monetary gifts, dividends, proceeds from the sale of a house, and money we win, inherit, or find on the street. Everything! All financial income! And when in doubt, I still tithe. No matter through what channel it came, its origin is God.

Do I have any say in how my tithe may be used?

No. You must tithe without any attachment. How the person or institution cares to use the tithe is up to them alone. You cannot say, for example, "Don, here's my tithe. I want you to go out and buy some gold-rimmed glasses." Instead you should say, "Don, you have fed me spiritual food. Thank you very much." Period.

In addition, you do not make moral judgments on that person or institution. For example, if you received spiritual food from an organization that does not recycle and you are an avid environmentalist, do not make a judgment and with-hold your tithe. They gave you spiritual food, so you must give them a tithe.

Perhaps you wish your church would use your tithe to clean the stained-glass windows that you look at every Sunday morning instead of just putting it into the building fund. Too bad. You give your tithe, and how the board of directors of the church then chooses to use the tithe is none of your business. If those windows are really bothering you, you could always give a little extra money over and above the tithe to have them cleaned, or you could always offer to clean them yourself.

How do I tithe on gifts, lunches, free tickets, and so forth?

Keep in mind that there is really no such thing as personal property. Gifts, then, are yours to use and enjoy and pass on when you are through with them. You are the temporary steward of property. Enjoy and share! It is not necessary to tithe on lunches, free tickets, or gifts (unless they are monetary). Only money needs to be tithed on.

Did Jesus teach tithing?

Jesus did not need to teach tithing because it was so much a part of his religious heritage that it was taken for granted that one tithed.

How do I overcome my fear of tithing?

We move through our fears by doing. Just tithe, in spite of your fear, and hold to the promise that the windows of heaven are opening for you and that you are proving that God is the source of your good. Find another person with whom you can pray. Listen to tapes and CDs. Read spiritual books that comfort you. Talk to other people who tithe and let their stories inspire you. Pray. Study. Believe.

Is it okay to tithe 1 percent or 5 percent? Do I have to tithe 10 percent?

Since the word *tithe* means *10 percent*, anything less is not a tithe and does not fulfill the law.

How can I tithe when I can't even pay my bills?

Do not allow your fear to paralyze you and keep you stuck in being less than you are. Tithe first and trust God to assist you in paying the bills. Be responsible about money and refuse to create debts that you feel guilty about. Ask for wisdom. Read Malachi 3:10 over and over and make a new choice to believe. The truth is, unless you tithe, you probably will never be able to pay your bills. After all, if you can't tithe on the piddly amount you have right now, do you think God is going to trust you with lots more? We have to be

trustworthy in the small matters before we can become
masters of the great ones.

*Can I be excused from tithing? I'm retired (on welfare, unem-
ployed, in school, etc.) and on a fixed income.*
In God's mind, there's no such thing as a fixed income.
Besides, if you consider yourself on a fixed income, it is
because you fixed it with your belief system.

No one is excused from obeying spiritual law. Lack of
faith will cause you to justify not tithing, but that thinking
will keep you from your unlimited abundance. Affirm
instead that your good is unlimited.

How do I know where to tithe?
Ask in prayer, "Where have I received spiritual food? Where
does this tithe go?" Then follow the guidance that you receive.

*Does it somehow diminish the tithe if I can deduct it on my
income tax return?*
No, I don't believe so. If you can legally deduct the tithe,
then you have more money to give elsewhere. And all giving
is good.

Isn't it sinful to be so concerned with money?
I believe that money is a spiritual symbol of invisible spiritual substance. Money is not evil, but a lot of people get
stuck on the concept that it is. In our Puritan ethic, we've
been taught that money is the root of all evil. But I don't believe that's true. I think it was Mark Twain who said, "The

lack of money is the root of all evil." Doesn't that make better sense? I mean, if you had plenty of money, would you steal? Of course not. It's a *lack* of money that causes people to do bad things. And it's when we begin to love money more than our integrity that we begin to have problems.

God doesn't want you to be poor. God wants you to have everything. God has put you here on this Earth so that you may have it all—if you are *willing* to have it all.

What about people who don't tithe and prosper anyway?
As I described in the Introduction, prosperity includes the following:

- A vitally alive physical body to provide a comfortable worldly home for the spiritual beings that we are
- Relationships that are satisfying, nurturing, honest, and work all the time
- Work that we love so much that it's not work, it's play
- And all the money we can spend

While there may be those who don't tithe and yet have big incomes, simply having money alone is not true prosperity. We need to be cautious about judging others' levels of prosperity based upon the part of their lives that we can see. Besides, it is really none of our business how or what they are doing, anyway.

Charles Fillmore says in *Prosperity*, "Tithing is based on a law that cannot fail, and it is the surest way ever found to demonstrate plenty, for it is God's own law and way of giving."

God wants to open the windows of heaven for you, too, to shower your life with abundance. You give yourself permission to receive this abundance when you tithe.

Try it! God says. *Let me prove it to you!* In the next chapter, we will make a plan for you to start tithing, so that you can finally give God a chance to make good on this promise.

CHAPTER 3

TITHING IN YOUR OWN LIFE

Just by opening your mind to the concept of tithing as a cornerstone of a prosperous life, you have taken the first essential step in your own spiritual journey. But as with all other principles in this book, tithing doesn't work if you just read about it, think about it, and talk about it. Tithing will work in your life only if you actually do it.

Most people's thinking about God and faith takes a sharp turn when it comes to money. They want their religion to stop at their hip pocket, not wanting their checkbooks or wallets involved. They rationalize this by saying that God knows and cares about everything except money.

But nothing could be further from the truth. In fact, if you want true prosperity, you must put God *first* in your finances. And it may be scary to do that. But once you move through the fear of tithing and you get to the other side and have proved God in your life, I promise you'll discover that you love to tithe. Absolutely love to! You'll find you can't wait to get some more money in so you can send some more out.

When I first started tithing, I got paid once a month.

That meant one lump sum to tithe on. Now, money comes into my life so rapidly I have to tithe nearly every day. I love it. And so will you.

GOD IS YOUR SOURCE

Now that you understand what tithing is all about, it's time for you to try it for yourself. When you think about tithing for the first time, you may hesitate, feeling that you just don't have any extra money to give away. You may worry about all the bills that will be coming in and wonder how you will be able to pay them. Well, don't you think God knows about those bills? Trust me; God isn't going to leave you high and dry. We must believe that God will show us how to meet our obligations.

Perhaps you hesitate to tithe because you have a lot of money in the stock market, and you wonder what would happen to your finances if the market crashed. Or maybe you fear losing your job. But the stock market isn't your source, and neither is your job. God is your source! Go ahead and say it out loud: "God is my source!"

If you have faith that God truly is your source, you don't really need to worry about what's going to happen in the stock market or whether you're going to lose your job. All you have to be concerned with is your relationship with God. It's a delusion to think that you are in charge of your financial life by what you do each day, such as landing a big account at work or putting money into your 401(k). People's fortunes can change in a fraction of a second, for good or for bad, by winning the lottery or by a devastating accident. God is in charge—not your boss, your broker, or your CPA.

My wise granddaddy once told me when I was a child, "Edwene, honey, when you have to swallow a frog, it's best not to look at it too long. And if you have to swallow more than one, swallow the big one first."

Tithing is the big frog for many people, so I urge beginning tithers to take my granddaddy's advice and not look at it too long. (That big ole frog is not going to get any prettier!) Don't overthink it. Just make tithing one of your spiritual practices, trust that the Scriptures are true, stand on the promises, and watch with wonder as the windows of heaven open to you.

> "If we could read the secret history of our enemies, we should find in each man's life sorrow and suffering enough to disarm all hostility."
>
> —Henry Wadsworth Longfellow

Wherever you are in consciousness right now, start to tithe. Don't wait for the right moment; do it now. Today. It's not a thing that you have to think about, or debate, or consider, or talk to your friends and family about. Just do it. And don't just do it one time and say, "Well, nothing happened." After all, you wouldn't tell your trainer at the gym, "I worked out one day, and it didn't work. I can't see a difference."

What will happen after you've been tithing for a while is that supply will start to come from all sorts of strange places you would never have expected. And the income will just keep increasing, from people and places you couldn't have planned for.

When this starts to happen, human nature is to ask, "How can it be that all this good stuff is happening to me? How can this possibly occur?" The truth is that the how and why of it are none of your business. "How" is God's business, and you couldn't figure out how if you spent a thousand years trying. Because God has infinite ways of bringing your good to you. Instead of wasting your time trying to figure it all out, work on shifting your consciousness toward trust that there will always be enough, and that you will always be provided for.

TITHING IS NOT CHARITY

When you first start to tithe, you may assume that you should give your tithe to charity. But that is not true. In fact, many mystics believe that if you tithe to *need*, you *create* need in your life. (This is not to say that you should not give to charity—all giving is good. What is important is that you tithe first. Then, after you've given your 10 percent, you can consider charitable giving.) Giving to charity is a very kind and generous thing to do, but it isn't a tithe.

A lot of people tell me, "I like to support good causes in the world." Well, that's fine. By all means, they should feel free to do that. But, that's not a tithe. That's over and above a tithe. Wonderful! But, that's not a tithe. Other people will say, "I help my Aunt Betty. She's having financial difficulty." Good for you. If I knew Aunt Betty, I'd help her, too. But, again, that's not a tithe.

A tithe is one-tenth of all income given back to where you receive your spiritual food in order to acknowledge that God is your source. And instead of tithing to need, you must tithe to abundance—in order to bring abundance into your life.

How can you know when you are being spiritually fed? Spiritual food is that which inspires you, lifts you up, and lets you remember who you are. It gives you a boost, a feeling of hope and inspiration. It brings you joy, and you know you're living your divine purpose when you experience joy. Start keeping a journal or notebook so that when you feel inspired or enlightened, you can write down who or what was the source of that feeling. Then, as money comes into your life, you'll know where to send it back out to.

Let me repeat that when I say we must tithe to where we receive spiritual food, I am not saying it must be to a church or a minister. Perhaps it will be, but then again, maybe you get your spiritual food elsewhere. In my life I have found that I have had all kinds of spiritual teachers, and they didn't all look like ministers. And some of them were a long way from a church.

One time I tithed to a waitress. I was sitting in a coffee shop and my life was in the pits. You know the pits? You ever been there? At the time, I was involved with someone who had an addiction problem, and it was frightening to realize how powerless we were in the face of it. My inability to help either him or myself was making me feel hopeless, and I was in terrible emotional pain. Whatever spiritual truth I ever thought I knew, I had forgotten.

> "We must be willing to get rid of the life we've planned, so as to have the life that is waiting for us. The old skin has to be shed before the new one can come. You can't make an omelet without breaking the eggs."
>
> —Joseph Campbell

This lovely waitress kept coming over. She would pour me a cup of coffee, and she'd pat me on the shoulder, and she'd say something profound and uplifting. "God's brought

you this far, Honey," she'd say. "God'll get you through."
And then five minutes later she'd come back, and she'd pour
me another cup of coffee, pat me on the shoulder, and say
another little zinger. Well, about the third time she came
over, the light finally went on in my head. I said to myself,
"I can make it. Life's gonna be alright. I'm back in the
groove; I remember who I am!" It was wonderful.

So I wrote out a tithe check to her and told her, "My belief system says that I must tithe where I get my spiritual
food, and you just gave me a lot of spiritual food, so I want
to give this to you."

She started to cry. "I can't take that," she said.

"Whatever you do with this money is your own business," I told her, "but I have to give it to you."

Well, what I discovered about this beautiful lady, that
I would never have found out if I hadn't followed through
on my commitment to tithe, was that for six months out of
the year she worked as a waitress
not because she had to, but because
it was her way to reconnect with
and serve other people. During the
other six months she was a yoga
master and lived in an ashram. And
so, she had a chance to share her
philosophy on life with me—one that lifted me up when
I was feeling down and reminded me who I was, and that
life was worth living. And I had a chance to teach her about
the law of tithing. (So today she lives in a very fancy
ashram.)

"Reality is the leading
cause of stress amongst
those in touch with it."

—Jane Wagner

Of course, I have tithed to many wonderful religious organizations. I am not saying that you shouldn't. But I have also tithed to my massage therapist, because sometimes when she works on my body, emotional issues from old experiences come up. She is very intuitive, and she talks me through them and helps me gain insights and understanding. I have tithed to Greenpeace, not because they needed the money—which they doubtless did—but because the stance they took in a particular instance was so courageous, and that courage inspired and fed me. I once tithed to an author of a book that had brought me great joy and spiritual insight. (He immediately and fearfully returned my tithe, so he had obviously not positioned himself to receive from the universe!)

You might even tithe to a personal friend, if he or she has given you hope and inspiration. One time I even tithed to my daughter. As a little child, she came in and said something so true that I just had to tithe to her. So of course every day for the next six months that child ran around trying to feed me spiritual food.

As you can see, I enjoy tithing "on the spot." I keep a record in my notebook of what money needs to be tithed on, and I always have my checkbook or some cash on me in case I am unexpectedly fed spiritual food and want to tithe right there and then. However, you may choose to tithe differently. Some people enjoy deciding in advance where their tithe will go, so that they can look forward to giving the tithe when the money comes in. Others might enjoy routine and prefer to give all their tithes to one place, such as a church, through some automatic payment. You can feel free to tithe in the manner that best fits your personality. What is important is not *how* you tithe, but that you do it.

ALL GIVING IS GOOD

You must tithe, but over and above the tithe, you can give to anyone you want to, for any reason. I myself like to give to my family, my friends, my community, and many charities (including the Special Olympics, Habitat for Humanity, and the SPCA, among others). I love to share my abundance with them, and they love to receive it.

You are free to give as much as you want to. In fact, I encourage you to give more and more and more. Tithing is the beginning of giving, not the end. Tithing is baby-step giving. You start with baby steps, and then you learn to walk. And then to run.

Don't limit yourself to 10 percent; that's already God's. You really haven't even given anything away when you tithe. You've given to God what was already God's. Giving beyond your tithe is when you're truly giving.

Faith expands when you give. The more you give, the more faith you're going to have. You're going to find out that Emerson spoke true when he said, "You can't outgive God." There is a law of compensation: The more you give, the more you receive. God will provide it. One of my favorite affirmations is, "Everything I need is always at my fingertips." No matter what the situation, no matter what's going on, I need not worry because God will provide.

As you begin to tithe, practice living "deliberately," as Thoreau said. You may find it helpful and revealing to keep a journal in which you record all the money, gifts, surprises, and unexpected good that flows into your life for the first six months of tithing. The more good I noticed and appreciated in that first year, the more good I experienced. And when I tithed, I moved from fearful thoughts and anxious feelings like, "Will there be enough to pay the bills?" and "Can I really afford to do this?" into a gentle and tender awareness, a sweet assurance, a quiet knowing that the promises were, indeed, coming true for me.

I also remembered these words from the Bible:

- Ask, and ye shall receive.
- Fear not. It is the Father's good pleasure to give you the kingdom.
- Do not be afraid. Lo, I am with you always.
- I have come that you might have life, and live it abundantly.
- Give, and it shall be given unto you.
- As you give, so shall ye also receive.
- Call unto me, and I will show you great and mighty things that ye know not of.

If you are not tithing, go back and check your own financial records. You will clearly see that if you haven't been tithing, the universe has been getting its 10 percent one way or another. Maybe you had a car accident, or somebody stole something from you, or you sat on your glasses, or the dog chewed up your false teeth. While at the time they might seem like accidents, they aren't accidents at all. Instead, they're simply proof that tithing is not optional.

AS YOU GIVE, SO YOU RECEIVE

At one point during my journey toward prosperity, I decided that I wanted to receive more. I had a huge debt that I wanted to be free of, and I needed help from God to achieve that. Now, the further I went on my spiritual journey, the more faith and confidence I felt. Like everyone else, however, I also had my moments of uncertainty. When I decided my new goal was to become debt free, I felt unsure about how to proceed, so I asked God for a sign.

At the time I was looking for guidance, I was scheduled to speak at the Religious Science Church in St. Petersburg, Florida, and I was staying at a nearby hotel. And during my prayers I said, "Okay, God—I need a sign. Show me. What is the next thing that I need to do? I need a clear sign and I need it right now."

Well, I looked out the window of my hotel room and right outside was a huge billboard, a literal sign. It was from an international diamond marketing company and it said, "Raise your standard of giving." Isn't that wonderful? So I immediately began to raise my standard of giving. Whatever I was giving, I added another 25 percent to it. For example, if I was going to give $100, I would give $125 instead. And I still give on that level to this day.

Let me tell you what's happened as a result of that. In that hotel room, I made a clear-cut intention to be debt free in six months. And in the very first month, I was able to pay off three-quarters of my debt by raising my standard of giving. So much money flowed into my life that it was really unbelievable. I suddenly starting getting many more tithes (which I then tithed on), my workshops expanded with more giving attendees, and then I led a spiritual pilgrimage to Glastonbury that turned out to be quite profitable.

Now, you understand the law of giving is this: *As you give, so you receive.* That puts you absolutely in charge of your receiving. Are you ready to receive more? If you want to receive more, but don't know how to, here's the answer: Give more. Raise your standard of giving. I promise you that the results will be quite incredible.

PREPARE YOURSELF TO RECEIVE

Once you have been tithing for a few months, things are going to happen in your life. And you have to prepare yourself to receive them.

"Prepare myself?" you might ask. "I've been dying for more; I don't need to prepare myself." Well, the fact is that fear of success is even stronger than fear of failure, and the powerful and unexpected results of your new faith life can be downright scary. People can pray and pray for something, but then when the universe sends it along they become unnerved, and send it back.

You have to have the courage to claim that which is yours, dare to claim the good that God wants for you. One way is through affirmations. One of my favorites is, "I have wonderful gifts to receive, and I receive joyously." Try saying that out loud every time you start to feel nervous about all the new abundance that is appearing in your life.

On this spiritual pathway, you're going to get a lot of gifts. And you have to accept them all, because you bless the giver when you receive them. Even if you don't want them, you have to receive them. It doesn't mean you have to keep them—you can pass them along to someone else—but you do have to receive them.

In my first ministry, in Knoxville, one of the elderly women in the congregation came up to me one day and said, "I am making you a special gift for Christmas, and I just can't wait to give it to you."

Well, I knew that this woman was famous for making beautiful quilts, so I got all excited, thinking, *She's going to make me a quilt*. And every week she would come up to me after the service and say, "Oh, I worked some more on your gift, and I just know you're going to love it. It's really coming along now." Well, I just got more and more excited about it, and I just couldn't wait for Christmas, when I could snuggle under my beautiful new quilt.

Well, Christmas came, and the woman called me and said, "My son is here, and he has a flatbed truck. Could we bring your Christmas present over?"

> "Dark nights of the soul are extended periods of dwelling at the threshold when it seems as if we can no longer trust the very ground we stand on, when there is nothing familiar left to hold onto that can give us comfort. If we have a strong belief that our suffering is in the service of growth, dark night experiences can lead us to depths of psychological and spiritual healing and revelation that we literally could not have dreamed of."
>
> —Joan Borysenko

I was thinking what in the world has she made that has to be hauled over on a flatbed truck?

They came over, and I saw the son carrying a huge piece of plywood. Then he set it down and turned it around, and I saw that what she had made me was not a beautiful quilt, but a six-foot-tall portrait of a rooster, made entirely out of macaroni.

I was completely speechless.

I put the rooster in my living room for a couple of days, and I knew by looking at it that the Lord had laid a burden upon my heart. I also knew that there was somebody else out there in the world who really would love to have this rooster in her home, and so eventually I took it down to the Salvation Army so that that person would have a chance to find it and be delighted by it.

The point here is that you must receive, no matter what form the gift comes in. That rooster wasn't the right thing for me to have in my life at that particular time. But this lady was so pleased to give it, and I was so touched by the love that was behind it, and the great care she put into making it. She blessed me by caring enough about me to give me a gift, and I blessed her by receiving it.

REMEMBER, FAITH IS A CHOICE

Faith is a choice. You choose whether or not to have faith. People always come to me and say, "Gosh, Edwene. I wish I had your faith!" Well, then choose to have it! I choose to have this faith; it doesn't just happen. You make a choice about it. I choose to believe that the law of tithing is true. I choose to believe in God, and I choose to believe that God is my source.

Besides, what do you have to lose? You haven't been tithing so far, and you haven't been doing brilliantly, have you? Don't you want a life of riches and prosperity? At least be open-minded and willing to give tithing a try. Make a six-month contract with God, as I did. You have nothing to lose, and absolutely everything to gain.

Tithing is not the entire journey toward prosperity. In addition to returning one-tenth of all we receive to where we receive our spiritual food, we have to do our forgiveness work, we have to set our goals, and we have to seek, find, and get on our divine purpose—all of which we will explore in the chapters that follow. But first and foremost, we must tithe.

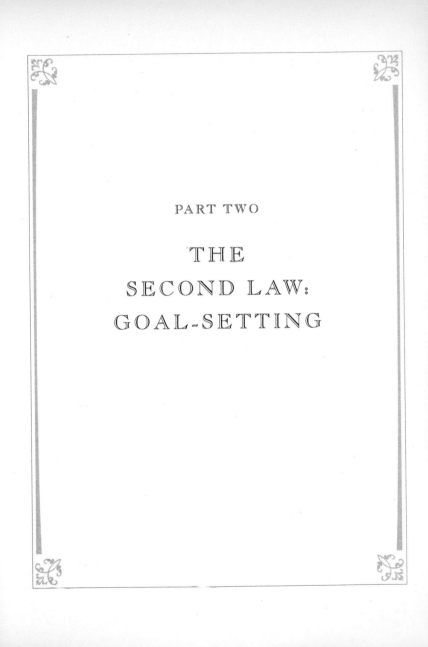

PART TWO

THE
SECOND LAW:
GOAL-SETTING

CHAPTER 4

WHY YOU MUST LEARN TO SET GOALS

In order to harness your new wealth and good fortune that tithing brings you, you must learn the next spiritual law: goal-setting. Goal-setting and developing directed faith can have truly spectacular results. Like tithing, however, goal-setting works only if you actually do it.

When you start tithing, the windows open and a shower of good starts flowing into your life. Now you need something to catch the good with, or it will be lost to you. Setting concrete and practical goals creates a vessel with which you can catch it.

During the process of goal-setting, you will need to take some time alone, away from the chaos and distraction of daily life, to get acquainted again with the real you. You may need to relearn how to daydream and let your mind wander, as you used to do as a child. Goal-setting is a wonderfully fun and creative part of the prosperity process. But it's also a very important one. You will need to give yourself the time and permission to dream big, or you will miss exactly what you are here for: to experience your own divine nature.

You're going to have to do some important inner work. I once heard a woman at one of my workshops say that she had to learn to "increase her bliss tolerance." I thought that was a great way to put it, and I myself am always looking for ways to increase my tolerance for pleasure. You have to get ready to accept what you want in your life.

And if you want something, you're going to have to get moving! You can't just sit there like a bump on a pickle. I'll show you how to get moving in this chapter. But before we get started, let's explore some of the essential elements of setting goals.

CASTING ASIDE YOUR LIMITATIONS

One of the main reasons people don't reach for their goals is that they believe there is something about themselves that will prevent them from getting whatever it is they really want in their deepest heart of hearts.

Perhaps you think you're too old to have all the things you really want. Or too young. You're too heavy, or too skinny. A woman, or of a minority group. Too tired, too broke. Married to the wrong person, or not married at all. But these statements are all lame cop-outs. And they aren't what's truly keeping you from getting what you want. While preparing to set goals, you must move beyond these limiting self-perceptions and step into the role of who you really, truly are.

And who are you? You are a child of God. You are an expression of the Most High. You are a point of light within the

Greater Light. Absolutely anything is possible that you want to achieve. But you've got to take concrete steps toward the dreams that you have. Goethe said, "Whatever you do, or dream you can, begin it. Boldness has genius and power and magic in it." And when you start moving toward your dreams, what you are going to find out is that God has so much more good in store for you than you could ever imagine. But before you can start receiving all the good God has in store for you, you must cast off a sense of your limitations.

Do you suffer from an illness that limits your mobility? Do you have a difficult family that thwarts your desires? Do you worry that your dreams are bigger than your bank account? Now is the time to put these things mentally aside and try to imagine what your life would be like if you could do anything you wanted, without any constraints and limits. Don't worry about how these things will come to you. The "how" of it is not your concern. God knows the "how." Instead, focus on asking yourself, "If money were no object, if time or responsibility or age or education were no concern, what would my life look like? What would the life of my dreams be?"

OPENING YOURSELF UP TO POSSIBILITY

Children think big. They plan to become famous movie stars, fly in spaceships to distant planets, conquer the world. They don't dream of becoming a stressed-out CPA, a struggling small-business owner, or an unhappy housewife.

As a child, you yourself thought big. Over time, perhaps scolded by parents, teachers, and siblings that you were a dreamer and should be more realistic, you probably began to shrink down your dreams.

Now, caught in the adult grind of daily chores—feeding the dog, picking up the dry cleaning, paying the bills—you may have completely lost sight of those early hopes and dreams. Now is the time to recapture the childlike feeling that the world is a rich and abundant place, and that you can do and be absolutely anything you want. It's time to learn to think big again.

BEING SPECIFIC IS CRUCIAL

Chances are you spend a lot of your time focused on other people's needs—perhaps your clients', your family's, or your friends'. Now it's time to begin to focus on what *you* want. Ask yourself, "What do I want?" Not, "What does my mama want for me? My kids? My spouse? My boss?"

"What do I want?" A lot of people have never even asked themselves that question. Or they asked themselves it once but then put the answer on the back burner for so long they've forgotten what it was in the first place. They are left with only a vague and blurry sense of what they want.

If you want to start effective goal-setting, where you are clearly conveying to God what it is that you want, then you've got to first get it clear in your own mind. After all, if you don't even know what you want, how can you ask God to send it to you? Can you imagine calling up a clothing catalog company and telling the person who wants to take your order, "Just send me something you think I'd like"? It wouldn't work at all. Instead, when you order clothing from a catalog you tell the person on the other end of the line what size, color, and style you want. Yet you dare to go before God with a vague attitude of, "I don't want to take the responsibility of choosing what I want, so I'll just take my chances and see what arrives." You can almost imagine God saying, "Here we go again. Another one unwilling to take responsibility for his or her choices."

LETTING GO OF SELF-JUDGMENT

Don't worry about whether you "should" want something. If you want it, you want it. And you don't have to say why you want it; it's enough to say that you just want it. When you're hungry for chocolate cake, you don't have to give a reason. You just want chocolate cake!

Besides, you're going to be keeping your list of goals private, so other people won't have a chance to pass judgment on what you want. It's none of their business, anyway. Your goals and desires are between you and God alone.

THE 21-DAY CHALLENGE

During this process of learning to set goals, I would like to introduce you to a life-changing exercise. When you set goals, you are going to prepare yourself to have and to do seemingly impossible things. To accomplish these remarkable things, you are going to need power, and you are going to need energy. And there's a simple way to get both.

A wonderful spiritual teacher of mine named Charles once taught me a beautiful lesson. I had been in Unity about three months, and by that time I thought I knew everything.

One Sunday after church I went up to Charles and said, "This church business is God's business, and it really needs to be done first class. I don't know who was responsible for vacuuming the Sanctuary today, but it was a mess. And I don't know who made the coffee, but it was so strong you could have floated a horseshoe in it. And the soloist was completely off-key—we can't ever have her again. And there were at least six typographical errors in the bulletin." And I went on and on.

This great, high, holy teacher patiently listened to my long litany of complaints. Then he said, "Edwene, dear, for you today, the highest metaphysical law in the universe is, 'Don't bitch!'"

I was taken aback. That wasn't at all the response I had expected. So I went home and prayed about it. I prayed, "He doesn't appreciate what I was trying to do. I was just trying to help."

And then I heard the little voice inside me, the one that always speaks the truth, and it said, "You should pay attention to what he said."

I had once heard somewhere that if you do anything for 21 days, it will become a part of your soul. I didn't know if that was true or not, but 21 days sounded like a period of time that I could work with. So, I made myself a 21-day calendar, which I posted on my refrigerator. And I made the commitment that for 21 days I would not gossip, I would not criticize, I would not complain—not to others or even to myself (if I could help it). I would not utter any negative language at all for 21 days. No matter what happened during that time, whatever disaster might befall me, my response was going to be, "Well, that's great." And I marked off those 21 days as they passed on my calendar.

> "See, the human mind is kind of like . . . a piñata. When it breaks open, there's a lot of surprises inside. Once you get the piñata perspective, you see that losing your mind can be a peak experience."
>
> —Jane Wagner

Now, I had always thought of myself as a wonderful conversationalist, always ready for some witty repartee, and that I always had interesting and entertaining things to discuss with the people around me. But for the next 21 days, I could not think of a single thing to say.

During that time I took a real good look at Edwene, and I was not very tickled with what I saw. I saw that I was a poisoner who was poisoning my own environment with gossip. I saw that I was a murderer, because sarcasm is murder. Criticism is murder. Gossip and criticism create a powerfully negative energy that really pollutes everything around you.

At first, when I stopped complaining and criticizing, I couldn't think of anything to say. I just didn't know what to do with myself. But, then, after some time had passed, I found that I had all sorts of new energy pouring into me. It was what we call in the old school "Holy Spirit power."

All of a sudden I had so much more energy and time to contribute to the good ideas and projects in my life. And I began to experience the joy that comes with praising and saying good things about other people, and appreciating more what I had in my life. (Because it's a spiritual truth that the more you notice the good in your life, the more you get. The more you notice even the small things—a beautiful sunset, a penny on the street, the pretty flowers in the park— the more you get. The more you notice the gifts God gives you, the more God gives.) And with this new joy I was experiencing came a great sense of power. I got to experience what it feels like to be truly powerful.

> "The ascent to the bright peaks of true being is always preceded by a direct descent into the dark depths. Only if we venture repeatedly through zones of annihilation can our contact with [the] Divine Being, which is beyond annihilation, become firm and stable."
>
> —Karlfried Graf von Dürckheim

Are you willing to be powerful? Are you willing to harness the energy that will propel you forward in reaching the goals you set for yourself? If so, I invite you to start by taking the challenge of not complaining for 21 straight days. No criticism, no bitching, no gossip. None. And if you slip and say something negative, you have to forgive yourself, and then start all over again for another 21 days.

So on the 20th day you must be very, very careful!

When you have fasted in this way for 21 days, you are going to find out exactly how powerful a being you are. Power is your birthright. And power is what you need to accomplish great things. But first you must be faithful in small matters before you'll be made a master over great matters. I invite you to prove to the universe—and to yourself—that you are the being of integrity that God made you to be. One that does not complain.

GIVING UP WHAT YOU DON'T WANT

When you are working toward your goals, not only do you need to know what you want, but you also have to be willing to give up that which you don't.

A young woman named Lisa called me because she just hated the job she was in, and yet she couldn't bring herself to leave it. She desperately needed the money and did not think she could find another job. Feeling trapped and miserable, Lisa said she didn't know what to do. Knowing the power it has to change lives, I started her on the 21-day "no complaining" challenge and gave her several affirmations to use.

Much later, Lisa called to tell me that she did the 21 days faithfully. Then, on the morning of the 22nd day, when she went into work, her boss attacked her physically. Shocked and frightened, she grabbed her things and ran out. All morning, she drove around in her car absolutely hysterical, crying and shaking, trying to remember any of the affirmations I had given her, and the only one that she could remember was, "I choose to live in trust." Lisa kept repeating this to herself, and finally she had calmed down enough to stop the car. She went into a diner for a cup of coffee.

There weren't many people in the diner, and the waitress was very kind. The person who had been in the booth before

Lisa had left a newspaper behind, and as she sipped her coffee she picked the paper up and started looking through it. There Lisa saw an ad for a job that she thought she could do. She went to the pay phone and called, and the woman said, "Come right over. We're interviewing right now."

The job seemed perfect for Lisa; the location was beautiful, the offices were pleasant, and the people who interviewed her were nice and friendly.

The woman who was interviewing Lisa said, "You sound great, but I have several other people I need to interview. We'll be in touch." Lisa was disappointed because she wanted the job so much. But when Lisa got home, her phone was ringing, and it was the woman, saying, "I don't know what I was thinking. You're absolutely perfect for the job. How soon can you start?" And Lisa started the very next day, at twice her previous salary.

The lesson of this story is that when you don't move voluntarily, the universe will give you a swift kick in the derriere to get you going. Because Lisa couldn't find a way to leave a situation that was bad for her, the universe had to throw her out. After all, she couldn't start the great new job until she'd gotten rid of the old one. You have to be willing to give up what you don't want in order to get what you do.

WHY IT'S GOOD TO HAVE GOALS

Before you start goal-setting, you must first accept the premise that it is not only acceptable to have desires, it is necessary. In his book *Prosperity*, Charles Fillmore states that "desire is the onward impulse of the ever evolving soul." It stands to reason then that if we are evolving souls (and I believe that we are), then our desires—the longings of our hearts—are what propel us forward into the life experiences required for an evolution of consciousness.

Many wise souls before us have recognized that we must grow or die. Christians commonly recognize this as the injunction given to us by Jesus, when he said, "Ask, and ye shall receive." We all want to receive the good God has in store for us, and goal-setting is the way to position ourselves to receive.

So let's get started. For the past thirty years, I have been working with and developing what I call my own personal goal-setting program. I put it into a ten-step formula that has proven wonderfully successful for me. Those ten steps are as follows:

Step 1: In a notebook dedicated to your goal-setting program, write down all of your desires, no matter how large or small.

Start by just writing down some things that sound fun to do, even if they sound silly or far-fetched. For example, you might jot down that you'd like to "hike through the Scottish moors," "have lunch with the Dalai Lama," or "do stand-up comedy." Always carry your notebook with you, so that as you think of new and appealing things during the course of the day, you can jot them down. Simply writing down your ideas will send a powerful message to your subconscious mind that the world is an abundant place and that all things are truly possible.

Step 2: Choose your most important desires and list them in order of importance to you. Be very specific.

I like to work with 12 at a time. When listing your specific goals, make sure that they are your goals, not your daddy's goals for you, or your spouse's or boss's. (You can tell when your goals are truly your own because they make your heart sing when you think about them.) Write your goals down clearly and specifically. For example, do not write as a goal that you want to "go on vacation." You might say instead, "This summer I want to fly to Austria for glacier skiing and yodeling lessons in the Tyrol." If you cannot be that specific, it may be an indicator that it isn't yet time to set a vacation as a concrete goal.

Once you have a goal in mind, you can start taking steps to get ready right away. For example, if your goal is to go to the Loire Valley, get your passport. Get a language book out of the library and brush up on your French. If your goal is to get married, go buy your wedding dress. Don't wait until the last minute! Start getting ready now.

Ask yourself, "What action could I take that would show I mean business?" Then take it. Doing so will send a clear message to your subconscious, and your subconscious will say, "Wow, she really means business this time. We'd better get cracking."

Step 3: Consider what changes you might need to make in order to achieve your goals.

During this step we must ask ourselves prayerfully, "What must I change about myself in order to achieve my goals?" This is where most people lose their nerve and abandon the process, because honest self-appraisal can be difficult.

If you ask this question with authenticity, you will get an answer. It may, however, not be the answer that you'd hoped for. For example, it may suggest that you better yourself by going back to school to get that degree, joining an exercise program and losing weight, taking voice lessons and singing a solo, or joining Toastmasters and learning how to speak in public. But whatever the answer is, if you are truly open to hearing the answer and making the necessary changes, you can have what you desire.

Step 4: Choose the date by which you desire to achieve each goal.

Putting down a specific date is a strong statement of confidence in both yourself and God. Now that you've realized you want to go to Europe, get married, or get a Harley, you must decide when (making sure, of course, that the date is one that you can genuinely believe in—not, for example, that you will lose thirty pounds in a week).

If you set a date that makes sense to you and the goal does not show up by that point, you must do another self-appraisal, telling God, "You probably told me what I need to change, but I wasn't listening closely enough. Please tell me again. I am paying better attention this time."

Step 5: Read your list of goals at least three times every morning and every night.

Reading your goals every morning and night gives them the powerful quality of affirmations. It also keeps them in the forefront of your mind, so that you never lose sight of them and return to your previous, limited way of thinking.

But there's more to it than that. When you focus on something, you draw power to it. There is a metaphysical law called "The Law of Mind-Action" that states, "Thoughts held in mind reproduce after their own kind." So when you keep a goal in mind, you are reproducing it, and drawing energy toward it.

Step 6: Imagine yourself achieving each goal.

Since you have defined your goals in specific detail, you should be able to picture them clearly. Imagine yourself driving the red VW convertible with white leather seats and shiny chrome hubcaps. Picture yourself snorkeling among the sea turtles in the bright blue water off the coast of Maui. The more regularly you envision yourself having the things you want, the easier they'll come to you, and the more able you'll be to actually accept them when they manifest themselves in your life.

Step 7: Act as if you have already achieved your goals. Believe that you receive.

Acting with confidence and faith in yourself and your potential sends a powerful message to the universe. Accept your success right now. Don't wait until you have actually achieved results. Act *as if.*

If you want a new home, go talk to a realtor and look at homes. If you want to go on a cruise, drop by a travel agency and pick up a brochure. If you want to get married, start looking at places where the ceremony could be held. Taking positive action toward your goals while radiating confidence in your ability to achieve them will catapult you forward in your journey.

Step 8: Don't tell others. Keep your goals private, between you and God.

When you are going through the process of goal-setting, privacy is key. Like the other spiritual laws, goal-setting requires a leap of faith that might be criticized by those not familiar with the process, thereby planting doubt in your mind and possibly causing you to stray from your new path.

It may be, however, that you have a prayer partner who understands your new journey to prosperity and who will be supportive of your goal-setting. If this is the case, by all means confide in that person (and offer to listen to his or her goals, too). But unless you feel confident you will be encouraged and supported, don't ask others' opinions of your goals and don't try to get their approval of what you are doing. Your list of goals is between you and God.

Step 9: Cross off the goals as they are achieved and continue to add new ones.

Dreaming and setting concrete goals should not be a one-time event, but a continually ongoing process. The more we practice the habit of tapping into our hearts' desires, the more easily we can expand the sense of possibility in our lives and aspire to greater heights.

Remember, there are only two things ever going on in the universe at all times—circulation and congestion. If we don't make new goals, we are telling the universe, "Don't send me new dreams." But by crossing off old goals and adding new ones, we invite a continual flow of goals and achievement into our lives.

Step 10: Remember, God's highest law is LOVE.

During this process, we have been goal-setting without thought to our financial constraints, our physical limitations, or the current state of our lives. That is because the only thing we really have to keep in mind when setting goals is that God's highest law is love. God wants the best for us, always. With this in mind, why should we worry about anything else? Our job is to learn to love ourselves as God loves us. Only then can we truly love our neighbors.

Remember—with God, all things are possible!

THE MESSAGE HAS BEEN SENT

Once I have taken each of these steps and seen the process through to completion, then it is time for me to put my trust in God that it will happen (while continuing to take action toward the goal and to act as if I have already achieved it). I myself pray for what I want in a lot of different ways. I affirm, and I ask out loud and silently, saying, "This is what I want." I write out my affirmations. I visualize and make treasure maps. I keep praying until I get that little internal click that says, "It's done," that inner knowing that the message has been sent.

Once I have clearly explained to God exactly what I want, and I have the sense that the message has been sent, then I let go. And then while I am waiting for what I want to manifest itself in my life, I ask again, "Is there anything I could or should do?" I want to make sure I stay in tune to the possibility more might be required on my part. (But when I do I'm not asking, "Well, where is it?" It's like ordering something from Neiman Marcus. Once you've called and placed an order, you don't keep calling the company back every fifteen minutes, saying, "You *are* going to send it, right?" Once you've put in the order, you can trust that it is on its way.)

MY FIRST EXPERIENCE WITH GOAL-SETTING

The first time that I myself made a list of goals, my most important goal was that I wanted to go to Mexico City. I'm not sure exactly why I wanted to go; I just wanted to. I wanted to see the Pyramid of the Sun and the Pyramid of the Moon. I wanted to walk in the marketplace and hear the mariachis play. I wanted to see the paintings of Diego Rivera. I wanted to eat fresh tamales and practice my Spanish. I really wanted to go! But I had no money.

Putting a trip to Mexico down as one of my goals felt like a real joke, because at the time I couldn't even pay my electricity bill. Obviously, taking a trip South of the Border was out of the question. But I had been told to write out my goals, and I'm good at following instructions. And besides, I was trying the system out for the first time, and wanted to see if it actually worked. So I wrote down, "I want to go to Mexico City by October 31."

I visited a travel agent and made a reservation. I made my reservation three months in advance so that I would have plenty of time to try to rustle up the $200 fare. I reasoned that the worst thing that could happen would be that I wouldn't get the money and that I would embarrass myself in front of the travel agent. Well, I've been embarrassed before. I knew I could take it.

I tried to get ready to go to Mexico City and did all the things my spiritual teacher at the time told me to. As she'd instructed, I said affirmations about traveling easily and effortlessly, I did visualizations about being there, and I thanked God in advance for the trip. But I still had the feeling that I was not going to go to Mexico City. And I knew that was a problem. Because, as Charles Fillmore suggests, you can think something until you're blue in the face, but you're not going to have your demonstration—the appearance in your life of that which you want—until you *feel* it!

When I went to my teacher for guidance, she told me, "Edwene, the problem is that you're not feeling rich."

"Well, of course I'm not feeling rich," I told her. "My bank account is almost empty. 'Feel rich!' What are you talking about?"

"You know exactly what I'm talking about," she said. "You're not ever going to *be* rich until you *feel* rich. Go out today and buy something for yourself at the level you can afford that makes you feel rich."

Well, in those days the level at which I could afford wasn't very much. But I also knew she was right. There's always something that can make us feel rich. And I knew just where I felt the poorest.

My biggest money issue at the time was in the grocery store. When it came to buying food, I was the world's biggest tightwad. I was the kind of shopper who made her menu for the week and then bought only what was on the list. And I bought only the basics: beans, cornbread, flour, peanut butter—no frills. And if we ran out, that was too bad. We ran out. We didn't go back to the grocery until the next week.

My teacher suggested, "Go to the grocery store and buy something that makes you feel rich." Just the thought was scary to me, but I went into my local grocery with my little rigid list, as usual, and this time I asked myself, "What could I buy here that would make me feel rich?"

I went to the gourmet section of the store and saw some jars of olives that had almonds in them. They looked so good! A jar cost $1.29, which completely blew a hole in my food budget. I can remember looking at the olives as if they were solid gold. But I put them in my shopping cart anyway because I was just sure they were what rich people ate.

And I felt rich. Sort of. I went home and put my groceries away, and then I called my girlfriend Lana, who lived in an apartment complex that had a swimming pool.

"Lana," I told her, "I'm coming over there and bringing a little bottle of olives with almonds in them, and I want you to get out that bottle of wine you have in your refrigerator, and your new wine glasses, and your little crystal bowl. We're going to sit at your pool and drink your wine, and we're going to eat these olives with almonds in them, and we're going to pretend that we're in Mexico City!"

Lana was pretty surprised. But she loves me, so she went along with it. I went over to her place with my olives, and she served her wine. And we sat by the pool, eating and drinking and pretending we were in Mexico City, saying, "Tomorrow we're going to the University of Mexico. And then, we'll go see the Pyramids. And the next day, we're going to the marketplace . . ." We were playing like children (which was okay, because unless you can become like a little child, you can't get into the kingdom, remember?).

We were very childish that day, and we had a lot of fun. I think we even got a little sloshed. But it was wonderful. In fact, we had so much fun that even though she didn't have any money either, Lana decided to go to Mexico City, too.

So she visited the travel agent and made a reservation. And then about a week later, Lana's mother bought her ticket. I was taken aback. After all, I was the one doing all the affirmations. I thought, "Where's *my* ticket?"

As the departure date drew nearer, I still didn't have a dime toward the $200 fare. I kept trying to stall the travel agent, but one day she telephoned and said, "Edwene, if you don't come and pay for these tickets today, I'm going to have to let someone else have them." I told her I'd be right over with the money. So I sat down and gave God a severe talking-to. I said, "Now, look here, God! I'm doing every single thing my teacher told me to do. I have been tithing and setting my goals. If there's something else I ought to be doing, show me and I'll do it. And if I'm doing something I ought not to be doing, then tell me and I'll stop. But, as far as I know, I have done every single thing that I know to do in order to manifest this trip to Mexico City. I've kept my part of the bargain. So now I'm going to go right down to that travel agent and when I get there, that money had better be there!"

I got in the car and headed out to the travel agent. On the way over, I got a notion to stop off and see my mother. Of course, deep down I hoped that if I told my mother about Lana's mother buying her ticket, then my mother might buy mine.

So I went in and acted really sweet, telling her about this wonderful plan of going to Mexico City that Lana and I had cooked up. Then I said, "Gosh, you know what? Lana's mother bought her ticket. Isn't that wonderful?"

"Why, yes it is!" my mother said. "What are *you* going to do?"

I could see that my plan was not working, so I went to leave. As I was going out the door, my mother asked if I would bring in the mail for her. She had a long driveway with a mailbox on a post at the end of the drive. And I walked out there grumbling and dragging my feet and kicking at pebbles, thinking, "Now what, God? Seems to me it's put-up or shut-up time."

I got the stack of mail out of her mailbox and started walking back toward the house, absently thumbing through her mail. Now, before I tell you what happened next, let me say that I hadn't gotten mail at my mother's in fifteen years. Nobody wrote to me at my mother's home, ever. But on that day, there was a letter for me. I didn't recognize the name or the return address. But it was clearly addressed to me.

When I opened the envelope and started reading the letter, I saw that it was from an old friend of mine whom I hadn't seen or heard from in well over a decade. She and I had once shared an apartment that we had furnished with pieces we'd picked up from the Salvation Army. After we'd lived together for a few months, I was notified that I'd gotten an overseas teaching job that I'd applied for. Since I knew that I was going to be moving into furnished quarters, I had left behind my share of the furniture when I moved out of our apartment.

In the letter, my friend wrote:

> *Dear Edwene,*
>
> *I don't know where in the world you are these days, but I found your Mom and Dad's name in the Houston directory. Do you remember all that stuff we bought at the Salvation Army? Well, I got married and have a new home, so I sold all our old furniture. And some of those pieces turned out to be quite valuable.*
>
> *I didn't feel right keeping all the money, since I remember it was kind of a struggle for us to pay for those things at the time. I felt it would only be fair of me to send you a check for half of what I got.*

The check was in the envelope. And it was exactly the amount I needed—$200! I simply couldn't believe it.

Needless to say, the experience was a loud and clear message to me about the power of goal-setting. And the story has an amusing postscript, too.

Lana and I had a wonderful time in Mexico City. But there was just one thing that put me out of sorts while we were there. Lana is what we in Texas call a "show pony." She's so pretty, with long, blonde hair. And Mexican men just love blondes. Everywhere we went in Mexico City, men gave Lana flowers. We walked down the street, and the men in a mariachi band stopped their playing, bought some gardenias, and gave them to Lana. We went to the marketplace, and a guy walked up and handed a big bouquet of flowers to Lana. Once, when we were riding the bus out to the University of Mexico, a man jumped on, gave Lana a flower, and then jumped off again.

One night, we decided to have our one fancy and expensive meal of the trip. We got all dressed up in our best clothes, went down to the dining room and sat at an elegant table with a beautiful linen table-cloth and napkins. Not sixty seconds had passed before a great big, long, white flower box—like the kind you see in movies—arrived at our table. It was filled with gorgeous, big, white orchids—for Lana, of course.

> "One thing that comes out of myths is that at the bottom of the abyss comes the voice of salvation. The black moment is the moment when the real message of transformation is going to come. At the darkest moment comes the light."
>
> —Joseph Campbell

I went immediately into prayer. I said—with clenched teeth—"God, I am really happy that Lana is getting all these flowers. But I really need a sign that I am loved, too. You've told me that I could ask for what I need, and I need a sign that I am loved, and I need it right now!"

At that moment, a waiter with a little towel over his arm came over and set down a small plate of hors d'oeuvres in front of me. And do you know what they were? Olives with almonds in them.

HAVING DIRECTED FAITH

What we are really doing when we are setting goals is di-recting our faith. Having directed faith means having a heart-felt specific desire, coupled with a deep and abiding trust in the goodness and generosity of God, and therein lies the magic and power of setting our goals.

Early in my studies, I came across a line in *Think and Grow Rich* by Napoleon Hill: "Directed faith makes every thought crackle with power." It reminded me of an important lesson I once learned from my little brother, Penn.

When I was a little girl, all I ever wanted was a pony. But my parents said no. They explained that horses were expensive, and they couldn't afford to buy one. So you can imagine my reaction when Penn came into my bedroom one day and said, "Guess what I'm getting for Christmas? A pony!"

"I've been wanting a pony all my life," I told him with annoyance. "I've never gotten one. What makes you think *you're* going to get a pony?"

With great exuberance he announced, "Santa Claus is going to bring me one!"

In my infinite wisdom at the ripe old age of twelve, I decided to enlighten him. I proceeded to tell him how the packages got under the Christmas tree, how all the gifts got in the stockings, and who really ate the cookies and drank the milk we left out. I ended with the pronouncement, "That's why you are not getting a pony for Christmas!"

Penn drew himself up, put his hands on his six-year-old hips, looked me straight in the eye, and announced, "That's what you think!"

I have to admit that his confidence shook me a little. I went to my father and asked, "Are you getting Penn a pony for Christmas?"

"No," he said, "We are not getting him a pony for Christmas. Leave him alone. He's just pretending."

Immediately I felt better. Penn was not going to get a pony, but as I watched him I noticed that my brother lived in a world where he was going to be getting a pony. He found an old Army blanket in the garage that he was going to use as his pony blanket. He dug around in the bathroom and found an old hairbrush he was going to use to brush the pony's mane and tail. He found an old washtub he was going to use for water for the pony. *My brother got ready for his pony.*

As I watched Penn, his confidence made me wonder. I went to my mother.

"Tell me the truth," I said. "Are you getting Penn a pony for Christmas?"

"No, Edwene, we are not getting him a pony," my mother assured me. "He's playing make-believe. Please, just leave him alone."

And so, I let it be.

As it happened, about two weeks before Christmas, my dad was invited to go on a hunting trip in South Texas with an old friend who was a rancher. Dad got up before dawn and drove to the ranch. As he and his friend were loading up the pickup truck for their trip, they heard a commotion in the stables and walked over to see what was happening. There they found a beautiful palomino mare giving birth to a palomino colt. The two men stayed to watch the holy birthing process.

As the colt was born, the rancher turned to my father and said, "Ed, you've been such a good friend to me all these years. Could I give this little colt to your son for Christmas?"

My dad was excited and stunned. He'd never mentioned Penn's obsession with ponies. Instead of going hunting, my dad got in the car, drove back home, and picked up my mom, Penn, and me to come and see the colt.

The colt was so fragile, with spindly legs that it couldn't get to work right. It was such a precious sight. I wish you could have seen the look of shock and happiness on my brother's face when he saw that little blond colt. And I wish you could have seen the pain and envy on mine!

> "Our work is to interpret this Life/Death/Life cycle, to live it as gracefully as we know how, to howl like a mad dog when we cannot . . . and to go on . . ."
>
> —Clarissa Pinkola Estés

The rancher was a very sensitive and understanding man. He could see what was going on inside me. So he came over and put his arm around my shoulder and said, "Edwene, I want your brother to have the colt, and I want you to have the mare."

Directed faith is not a vague, hazy, wishful yearning. It is a powerful belief of expectancy that causes the universe to send us wonderful things. There is no doubt in my mind that my brother's directed faith—which never wavered for one moment—brought us both our gifts.

WHAT ABOUT ASKING FOR NON-MATERIAL THINGS?

I'm asked this question a lot. People ask me, "Shouldn't our goals be non-material things such as 'having the peace of

God'?" And I suspect that many people want to put down an intangible because they think they *should* want it (which is the wrong reason to name a goal) and because they haven't yet learned to accept their real desires. And what's worse, that thing isn't usually even a real goal. For example, people say, "I don't really want more possessions. I just want peace of mind." Well, peace of mind is not a goal. Peace of mind is a choice. If you want it, just choose to have it. Or they say, "I want to be a more loving person." So, just choose to be one! There's nothing particularly hard about that.

A lot of people say, "Edwene, you're so materialistic. Why do you keep asking for all this stuff?" Well, I'm asking because my teacher told me to. What I know of Jesus the Christ—who is my guide and my model—is that he had the power to heal everybody who was on the planet Earth. While he was here he could have healed every single person had he chosen to. But do you know what he did instead? He healed only those people who *asked* him to (or those for whom someone else asked on his or her behalf).

Jesus said, "Ask and ye shall receive." He did not say, "Make me guess."

When people ask me, "Can I put 'more love in my life' on my goal sheet?" I tell them, "Honey, you've already got all the love that you are ever going to get." Sometimes people get depressed when I tell them that. But what they really need is not more love, but to be more aware of all the love that they already have.

You are a child of God. You already have all the wisdom, intelligence, faith, peace, and love there is. You're not going to get any more of that intangible stuff, so don't even bother putting it down. Why ask for something that you already have?

Besides, what if you put down, "more peace in my life," and more peace comes along in a form that you don't recognize, and you miss it completely? What a waste. But I can guarantee that if you put down "a bright yellow Lamborghini race car" and that sucker comes along, you're going to know it.

I had one woman who told me she wrote down as a goal at one of my workshops, "I want more love in my life." Then, when she got home, the neighbor gave her a pregnant dog! This woman got exactly what she asked for, but it was not what she *really* wanted. She should have instead written, "I want a baby," or "I want a new lover," or "I want to take a vacation with my five closest friends."

It's all about being specific, and about accepting your desires. Don't be ashamed of what you want or feel that you shouldn't have the desires that you do. Your desires are holy. You didn't make them up. They were implanted in you by God. I mean, why would people who come from similar backgrounds desire such different things, if God didn't implant those desires in them?

If you want a solid gold toilet seat, you've got a right to it. You don't have to justify your desires; you just have to accept them. In fact, for many people that's the biggest challenge—simply accepting their desires. To be able to say without hesitation, "Yes—that is what I want!"

Once I had gotten the hang of goal-setting, I decided I wanted to own a nice car. And not just any nice car, either.

I wanted to own a white Cadillac convertible with a white leather interior and a white top.

Of course, I didn't have the money to buy a Cadillac, but that didn't stop me from paying a visit to my local Cadillac dealer with my friend Lana. The only convertible they had was baby blue. I told the salesman, "I don't want baby blue. I want white on white on white. But I'll take it for a test drive and see if I like it."

I'd never been in a Cadillac before. Lana and I drove around with the top down, our hair blowing in the breeze. It was wonderful; we loved it. And I said, "Lana, I'm gonna have me one of these."

"But Edwene," she said, "it's so ostentatious."

"I don't care," I told her. "It's what I want. I don't have to justify my desires. If you want to stay in that little broken-down Mustang of yours, that's your business. I want a white on white on white Cadillac convertible." And six months from that day, my new husband gave me a white on white on white Cadillac convertible, completely paid for.

As well as having my own remarkable experiences with goal-setting, I've witnessed the countless experiences of the people I've worked with. One such person is a woman named Susan, who has graciously allowed me to share her story.

SUSAN'S STORY OF GOAL-SETTING

Susan and her husband attended a workshop I gave in California. When I said that a goal could be something really outrageous that a person would never think was possible,

Susan immediately thought of the Pillsbury Bake-Off Contest. Susan loved to cook and invent new recipes, and the Pillsbury Bake-Off Contest is the Super Bowl of cooking. Tens of thousands of people from across the United States enter, but only 100 finalists are chosen. Susan wrote down on her list of goals that she was going to be one of those finalists. (The challenge of tithing first before setting a goal was not a problem for Susan, since she and her husband had started tithing more than a year before they attended my workshop and were firm believers in the practice.)

Susan later told me that she read her goal of becoming a Bake-off Contest finalist three times every morning and night to keep it within her sights. With a full-time job as an accountant, Susan spent almost every evening and weekend furiously creating and testing new recipes. Some were pretty good after a few revisions; others went straight into the trash after the first try. Susan's husband had to sample so many versions of Raspberry Almond Pastries, he said he couldn't ever eat another one. For two straight months Susan worked as hard as she could, while getting ready to receive by imagining herself a finalist at the prestigious event. By the contest deadline, she had submitted twenty recipes.

One month later, Susan got a phone call telling her that her recipe for Chiles Rellenos Puffs, an appetizer she'd invented, had placed her as one of the 100 finalists. Susan became hysterical with excitement. She called her husband, but her voice was so high pitched with emotion and she talked so fast, not only could he not understand what she was saying, he didn't even know who the crazy woman was on the other end of the line! Once Susan calmed down enough to tell him her news, he was thrilled for her.

Now that Susan had achieved her goal of becoming a finalist, she decided to set a new goal. First, she wanted to win one of the 12 cash prizes. Second, she was concerned that she would get so nervous about the whole thing that she could ruin the experience for herself. So she wrote out the new goal, "I want to enjoy my experience at the Bake-Off Contest, make my recipe perfectly, and win one of the cash prizes." She read this goal three times every morning and night for two and a half months, until it was time to attend the event. Susan took action on her goal by making her recipe numerous times so that she would be more comfortable making it at the big event.

When she returned, Susan e-mailed me to say the Bake-Off Contest had been a success, just as she had imagined. She and her husband had met people from all over the country and been treated to three gourmet meals a day. She had a wonderful time and made her recipe perfectly. And then, to cap it all off, her Chiles Rellenos Puffs had won an "America's Greatest Cheese Recipe Award," which came with a $5,000 cash prize presented by Dick Clark at the event's award ceremony.

Now Susan has a new goal—to be the million-dollar grand prizewinner of a future Bake-Off Contest. But before Susan did anything else, she told me, she first tithed on the $5,000.

Now, just so that I am clear, I am not suggesting that if you ask for something from God you'll immediately receive it the same way that you put a dollar bill into a vending machine and promptly get a candy bar in return. It would be great if life and faith and prayer worked this way, but it doesn't, as illustrated by one last story I'd like to share with you.

MY SAFEWAY STORY

At one time in my life, when I had chosen to leave a marriage with a very wealthy man, I was once again broke. I had left the marriage with only $60 and the Cadillac convertible I've already told you about. At the time, I was in ministerial school, having made the commitment that I did not work for money. I worked for God.

I was in the bedroom, studying for my Bible comprehension exams. The amount of names I had to learn by rote for these exams was just staggering. But I wanted to do really well, so I was studying as hard as I could. Then someone started banging on the door. It was my daughter, who was 13 or 14 at the time, and she was just as mad as a wet hen.

She came into the room and said, "Look, Edwene. This is getting ridiculous. One of us has got to go to work! There is no food in the refrigerator, and I'm hungry!"

Guilt immediately came up. I mean, you're supposed to feed your babies, right? But I had nothing to give her. The $60 had been spent, and we couldn't eat the Cadillac. And the truth was I had been so busy doing my Bible work, I hadn't even noticed we were out of food. So, I said, "Okay, Honey. Give me a few minutes and let me do some prayer work on it."

"Great!" she said. "Pray about it. That's what got us into this mess in the first place."

She left in a huff, and I started giving God what-for.

"Look here, God!" I said. "I'm your lady! And I am doing everything I know to do. I am tithing. I'm not working for money. I'm teaching classes that people ask me to teach. I'm living off love-offerings. I'm doing everything I'm supposed to do. Now, listen up. I want some food in this refrigerator, and I want it right now!"

Just then, the phone rang. I picked it up and said, "Hello?"

"Congratulations!" said a voice on the other end. "You've just won $100 worth of food at Safeway."

I was so shocked that I could not speak for a moment. Then I said, "But I didn't even enter the contest."

"You're Edwene Gaines, aren't you?" he asked.

"Yes."

"Well, your name and telephone number are on this entry slip. We had a $10 winner, a $25 winner, and you're our big winner! Come right over and get your groceries."

"Defining myself, as opposed to being defined by others, is one of the most difficult challenges I face."

—Carol Moseley-Braun

Well, I was just beside myself. I came sailing out of that bedroom and right up into my daughter's face, and I said, "Praise God! Our prayers have been answered. We just won $100 worth of groceries at Safeway! Thank you, God! Thank you, God!!"

And she said, "Thank you, God, my foot! I stood for half

an hour at the table where they had entry slips and filled out 50 of those suckers!"

We've all heard the saying, "Be careful what you ask for because you just might get it." Well, that saying is wrong. Because there is no "might" about it. You'll always get what you pray for. It may come in a form you didn't expect or that you don't even recognize, in which case you might miss it entirely. Or, once you have it, you may realize that you don't really want it after all, and then you'll have to pray it back out of your life. But you're going to get what you pray for.

When it comes to getting what you want, sincere effort is required on your part. First, you must tithe faithfully on every dime you receive. Then, you must do your inner work to be open to the possibilities, to be specific in what you want, and to acquire a childlike sense of your own worth and your unlimited possibilities. You must develop *directed faith*. And finally, if you feel you're not getting what you've prayed for, you must be willing to enter into a truthful, prayerful, and thorough self-evaluation to see if there is anything about yourself that needs changing.

But above all other things, you must never lose sight of the fact that with God, anything is possible. By following both the spiritual law of tithing and the spiritual law of goal-setting, you can have anything you want, no matter how unattainable, extravagant, or outlandish it may seem. It will be God's great joy to give it to you.

CHAPTER 5

MOVING OUTSIDE YOUR COMFORT ZONES

Setting your goals is a great accomplishment, but actually taking practical steps toward them can be scary because that requires you to step outside your comfort zone. Everyone you know probably has a secret dream—like writing a novel or climbing the Matterhorn—that they have never pursued because doing so would mean changing the status quo of their lives. But you are on a journey—a journey of prosperity—and you are going to start accomplishing your goals, not just keeping them as secret dreams. So it is vital that you learn how to step outside the realm of where you feel personally comfortable.

As you start implementing the four spiritual laws into your life, things are going to start happening—perhaps in very unexpected ways. Change, even when it's for the good, can be frightening. But if you are going to transform your life through a journey to prosperity, you must try to learn to welcome change. And change inevitably requires that you be forced to move outside your comfort zones.

When you move outside your comfort zone, it is highly likely that you're going to feel fear. After all, fear is the invisible barbed wire fence that keeps us safely and securely within our comfort zones. But if you are going to live the life that God brought you here to live, you are going to have to learn to work through that fear because God has extraordinary plans for you. God wants you to walk on water. But before you can walk on water, you have to get out of your boat. You're too comfortable in your familiar little boat.

I believe that we all have big plans and dreams that we have not given ourselves permission to do. That will change for you as you read this book. In the meantime, before you can do the big things, it's okay to start with the small ones. Let's say, for example, that you want to learn how to fly an airplane, but you're too fearful. Well, perhaps you could start by taking a ride on that slightly scary-looking roller coaster at your local amusement park. Once you've gone for a spin around the track and noticed that you didn't perish from the experience, you might decide to try something a little bigger. And then something else a little bigger. Success is built through a willingness to play in an increasingly larger and larger arena.

One of the fundamental truths of human life is, "Grow or die." If you keep playing in your tiny arena, you're going to die of boredom. Your spirit will perish. As a human being and a child of God, you are designed to strive toward goals and solve problems. In order to do that, you have to do things you've never done before.

THERE IS NO FEAR IN ME

One of my favorite affirmations is, "There is no fear in me." Unfortunately, as many times as I say it, it is never completely true. I do have fear in me—a lot of it. We all do. And we have to learn how to work our way through it. I know that when I do a new thing, fear naturally comes up. And that's okay. Fear is something we may never be free of. However, we do have to learn the skill of moving through fear. We need to learn how to act in the midst of it.

Jesus knew how much fear we go through. He said time and time again, "Don't be afraid." And each one of us says back, "Yes, I know you said that. But still, I'm afraid."

When you have fear and do the thing anyway, you are holding on to the hand of God. Since you don't know what you are doing, you're sure glad God does. So many times I have crawled way, way out onto a limb of faith and prayed that God would grow a tree under me. And God always has. Have you ever noticed that on fruit trees, all the fruit is at the end of the limb? It's not up close to the trunk. You have to be willing to walk all the way out on that thin little limb in order to get the fruit. The same is true about God. If you wait for guarantees before you step out there on that limb, it's not going to work.

The people who succeed are the people who are willing to endure the fear, to act despite it, and not wait until the day (which never comes) that they feel no fear. For example, I have heard Olympic athletes who compete on the high dive say that even after years of training, it is still frightening for them to stand on the edge of that platform thirty feet up in the air. They say that the fear never goes away. Still, they do it. Because the only way to get the gold medal is by climbing up there and then going over the edge. You can't get the gold medal for diving if you stay on the ground.

For those of us who are trying to learn to live with our fear, I think a great way to start is to ask ourselves, "What is the worst thing that can happen?" I've heard it said, and I think it's true, that a lot of the rhetorical questions we ask ourselves when faced with risk (such as, "What if we get married and it doesn't work out?" "What if the stocks we're buying lose all value?" "What if the baby gets sick?") are not really questions, but simply expressions of fear. And the way to start moving through the fear is by answering those non-real questions as if they were real. What *will* you do if the marriage doesn't work out, or the stocks lose all value, or the baby gets sick? Because when you look at the worst-case scenario straight in the face, it loses much of its power to frighten you.

A lot of the time the worst-case scenario is simply that we'll fail and be socially humiliated. Well, being embarrassed isn't fun, but it's never actually killed anyone, as far as I know. In fact, failure is a wonderful teacher. When we fail we learn that we can survive the experience with all our faculties intact, and then we don't see failure as something really to be feared anymore.

One great tool is to learn how to say the word *Oops!* again. When you watch a baby learn to walk, she'll take a few steps and then fall; when she does, you don't say, "Look, you failed, you ignorant thing! Just stay down there and don't try again." Yet, this is what we often say to ourselves. It's a much gentler and more empowering thing to learn to say, "Oops! That didn't work. Oh well, I'll just have to try again."

Of course, we must take true risk seriously. But at the same time we have to remember that a lot of people who end up succeeding at a level we aspire to have often failed several times first. Lance Armstrong, for example, didn't even manage to complete the Tour de France the first time he rode in it. He dropped out; he failed. But he didn't let that failure stop him from becoming all that he was capable of being—the world-class, record-setting champion that God put him on Earth to be.

What did God put you on Earth to be? We all want to know the answer to this question. And the way we each find out is by stretching and stepping outside what we thought we could do. We learn to start discerning God's plan for us through stepping out of our comfort zones, taking risks, and learning to work through our fears.

MY CAVERN STORY

As a practical way to work on conquering my fears, every once in a while I schedule an activity that will scare the bejesus out of me. Not too long ago I decided that I was going to make a commitment to do something I wasn't sure I knew how to do— I was thinking about giving up my regular paycheck and starting a full-time seminar career with no guarantees of success, so I naturally started experiencing a lot of fear and anxiety. Feeling all that fear, I tried to think of a way to work through it. Then I came across some information on an eight-day workshop that was going to be held in Northern California. The whole eight days would be spent pushing through the fears and beliefs that limit us. Well, that sounded like just what I needed, so I signed up, paid the fee, then I flew to California.

Looking back, I have to say that I'm not sure what I was thinking when I signed up for that workshop. I suppose I thought that a bunch of us would spend a week in a lodge in the mountains of Northern California, taking nature walks during the day and gathering around the fireplace in the evenings. Maybe we'd open a bottle of Napa Valley Chardonnay, and then we would share with each other our most secret fears. We would look meaningfully into each other's eyes, do some forgiveness work, and then we'd all go home.

That wasn't exactly what happened. Instead, on the morning of the first day, all of us were loaded onto a bus and taken out to a cavern in the middle of nowhere. When we arrived we were informed that we were each going to rappel 200 feet down into the cavern to the bottom.

At that moment, every single ounce of spirituality and faith I thought I had flew right out the window. I am terrified of heights. I get dizzy just from standing on a step stool. Two hundred feet might as well have been two hundred miles; there was no way I was going to do it. I didn't know the people who were in charge, and there was no way I was going to trust them with my life. I was tensing myself, ready to make a run for it. Getting lost in the woods seemed a better fate than falling to my death.

The workshop leaders started giving instructions to the group. "When you step off this ledge, you're past the point of no return," they informed us. "There's only one way down, and it's all up to you. If you do not move this rope to lower yourself to the bottom, you will be hanging in space for the rest of your life." Then they gave me a little yellow hard hat. I couldn't believe they wanted me to put it over my carefully arranged hairdo. Imagine me in my gold lamé tennis shoes and polished pink nails, 200 miles from the nearest Saks Fifth Avenue, and these people urging me to put a hard hat on my head!

I started blabbering. "I can't do this. . . . There's been a mistake. . . . I don't want to be here . . ."

They didn't pay any attention. All the while I was explaining why I couldn't go over the edge of the cavern, they were hooking me up to a harness and putting gloves on my hands. In the meantime, one of the other people in the workshop, a man who was in the Navy, Air-Sea Rescue, walked around the cavern, whistling and looking delighted. I just wanted to smack the snot out of him.

Instead, I started to cry. The leader of the workshop came over and got right up in my face.

"Edwene, this is the first event of eight days!" he said. "If you do not do this, you cannot participate in the rest of the workshop. You'll be sent home and you will not get a refund!"

Well, finally, he had my attention. I had paid a lot of money to be there, and I was not going to let it go to waste. So I decided that I, Edwene Gaines, who had never done anything physical in her whole life, who had never broken a bone and never intended to, who was incapacitated with fear over the smallest of heights, was going to be going over the edge of a cavern with nothing but a rope and the certainty that I was about to wet my pants.

I can tell you without exaggeration that going over the lip of that cavern was one of the most frightening things I have ever done in my life. Carlos Castaneda, a writer I admire, said that fear is the blackbird that sits on your shoulder and tells you to pay attention. Well, as I went over the edge of that cavern I was paying 100 percent attention. In fact, I have never been so focused on any object in my life as I was on that rope as I stepped into air with nothing below me for 200 feet.

I began to lower myself down those 200 feet one inch at a time. And every time I moved that rope, I'd say, "Jesus . . . Christ! . . . Jesus . . . Christ!" When I was about halfway down, the people below, who had already lowered themselves down, were yelling up at me, "Look around! It's beautiful!" But I was in no mood for sightseeing. I kept focused on the rope, moving it inch by inch and muttering, "Jesus . . . Christ! . . . Jesus . . . Christ!" over and over.

When my feet touched ground at the bottom of that cavern, I just about fainted. I threw an old-fashioned southern hissy fit. I kissed the bottom of the cavern, I praised God, I danced and waved my arms in the air.

The man who was trying to unhook my harness was taken aback. "You alright?" he asked.

I was more than alright—I was a new person. The lessons I have learned from that experience continue to unfold and empower me every day of my life. Because what I knew about myself before that day was that if another person had been at the bottom of that cavern and needed me to come rescue him, I would have found a way to do it. There's no doubt in my mind. I would have found a way to get down there for him, because I would have known the inherent value of that person. But what I did not know was that I would go down there for me! To rescue the hurt child inside me that is still growing and healing and unfolding to be all that I came to be.

When I stepped off that ledge to rappel, I didn't trust that rope. I know I didn't trust myself. I certainly didn't trust the people that gave me the instructions, and I didn't even hear what instructions they gave. What I trusted was God. God took me into and through the scariest thing that I'd had absolutely no preparation for, and then God got me safely through and back out again. And each time you push yourself through your fears, you unfold that person within and take one step closer to being the powerful and unstoppable creature that you were brought here to Earth to be.

MY SHAMANIC HEALING

Not too long ago, I faced a new life challenge—I was getting ready to open my retreat center, and it was a big financial investment. I literally wasn't sure that I had the courage to do what I really wanted to do. So to move through my fears, I knew I had to face them head-on.

I decided to go to Ecuador to work with the shamans who are known for being shape-shifters. I flew to Latin America with a group of people I didn't know because I wanted to take the trip as a private citizen, not as a minister who would be counseling others.

After we landed, we drove up into the Andes, to a village that was 14,000 feet above sea level, where there was hardly any oxygen in the air. The shamans there call themselves "the bird-people." When we arrived three of them were waiting for us in their full ceremonial costume. Cecil B. DeMille himself could not have made them look more perfect for the part. They had tall, multicolored feather hats and paint on their faces.

As soon as I met the shamans, I felt that I had known them all my life—like they were brothers of mine. They worked with us for hours, telling us through an interpreter all about their herbal remedies, about how they talked to plants, and about shape-shifting.

It was absolutely fascinating, and I was so glad I had given myself the gift of taking the trip. Then the eldest shaman whispered something to the interpreter, who then announced, "The shaman would like to offer to anyone who would like it a healing."

Well, my hand shot right up into the air almost of its own volition. I didn't come all the way around the world to miss a chance. Of course, I wanted a healing. "Okay," they said. "You're first."

Hot damn, little ol' me from Valley Head, Alabama, was going to have a real, genuine shamanic healing. They took us to a special room with a dirt floor and a lot of interesting animal smells going on in it—I think they used the room to house goats. We all sat on tree trunks that they used as benches. Then the whole village came to witness the healing—all the neighbors with their kids and grandkids. As the room started to fill up I began to get a little nervous, with all these strangers and no idea what was going to take place. But then I happened to glance over at the wall and saw a tiny picture of Jesus Christ, which someone had tacked on the wall with a pushpin, so I knew I was going to be okay.

When everyone was gathered I went up in front to where the shamans were. They said something to the interpreter, and he turned to me and said, "Take off all your clothes."

I blinked, thinking, *Okay, well that's not going to happen.* Here I was surrounded by all these people, many of them young and attractive, and I myself was no longer a spring chicken, and maybe just a tad overweight. Well, to be honest, none of my body parts were in their original starting positions, and I was experiencing a lot of body shame. There was just no way I was going to strip nude in front of all these people.

I tried to think of a way out. I considered throwing my arms in the air, yelling "Praise Jesus, I'm healed!" and running out of the room. But I knew that wouldn't work. So I took a deep breath and asked my inner voice—my intuition, my guidance from God—what I should do.

"Isn't a new and challenging experience what you've come here for?" replied a voice in my head. "Isn't this exactly what you've traveled halfway across the world to do? Didn't you commit to moving through your fear? Didn't you agree to be healed?"

I thought for a moment.

"Is there anyone else in there?" I asked.

Well, of course I knew the little voice was right. So what I did was—in front of all those strangers, in front of that entire village—I took off all my clothes.

For the next hour and a half the shamans gave me a healing. What I experienced during the healing are things I am still trying to get my mind around. I saw fire breathed out of their mouths, and the flames surrounded my body. The shamans beat my body with rocks they call sacred stones. They whipped my body with stinging nettles. They blew into the top of my head, into my heart space, and I could feel their breath in my body. And I was healed, on some deep and profound level. I was healed of eons of body shame, and of a lifetime of guilt that I did not have the kind of body that the women in the fashion magazines have.

It was a powerful, astonishing, life-changing experience

that made me think of the line from Hamlet: "There are more things in heaven and earth, Horatio, than are dreamt of in your philosophy."

YOUR OWN JOURNEY

Today you are going to start thinking about some of the things that frighten you—especially those things you'd really love to do, that you have dreamed of doing, but that you were too fearful to do.

Please know that God wants you to do those things. God wants you to succeed because what you are in God's eyes is precious and adorable. God thinks you are just the sweetest thing that ever came down the pike. God wants you to have everything your heart desires. But in order to get it, you have to move through your fears and play at a higher level than you've ever considered playing before.

Working through your fear is all about taking the first step. In one of my workshops, we walk on hot coals. You move through fear the same way you walk on hot coals (which I have done hundreds of times). You pay attention, expect the best, and then you take the first step. The rest will flow naturally. Because once you've taken the first step and are on the coals, don't you think your body is going to know exactly how to get you back off again?

It's time for you to step outside the safety net you've created that you call your life, and take some risks. Learn how to work through fear. Doing so is an integral step in the direction toward becoming the person you were put on this

Earth to be. I invite you to try the following exercise to get you started.

STEPPING OUTSIDE YOUR COMFORT ZONES

Step 1. List five extremely scary things that there is no way you would ever do or even want to do (high-altitude ice climbing, BASE jumping off a tall bridge, going head-to-head in the ring with a heavyweight boxing champion).

1. _____
2. _____
3. _____
4. _____
5. _____

Step 2. List five scary things that you have always dreamed about doing but have never had the nerve to do (learning to SCUBA dive, participating in a poetry slam, living in a foreign country while learning the language).

1. _____
2. _____
3. _____
4. _____
5. _____

Step 3. List five small and only slightly scary things that you could do today if you chose to (asking your boss for the nice corner office that just opened up, trying sushi, inviting the good-looking neighbor whom you have a crush on over to your house for coffee).

1. _____

2. _____

3. _____

4. _____

5. _____

Step 4. Choose the most appealing of those five small things and write out what the first step would be to doing it (requesting a meeting with your boss, making a reservation at a Japanese restaurant, saying hello to the neighbor and introducing yourself).

_____

Step 5. Now, take that first step.

While the small first step you take may not seem like a big deal, it is. Because the hardest part is taking the first step. And the more things you accomplish in the list of small, easy things, the more likely you are to consider actually tackling one of the bigger things from the list of things you've always wanted to do. And once you've done one or two of those and learned the power of working through your fear and coming out the other side, who knows? Maybe you'll come to decide you actually want to try something from the list of things you swore you'd never, ever want to do. Like swallowing your fear and lowering yourself 200 feet down into a cavern, perhaps. And you have no idea the rewards that may be waiting for you at the end.

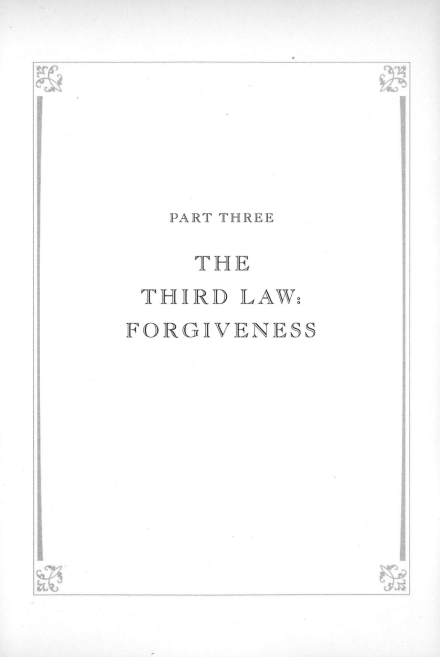

PART THREE

THE
THIRD LAW:
FORGIVENESS

CHAPTER 6

THE MYSTERIOUS POWER OF FORGIVENESS

Why should we forgive the people who have done us wrong? After all, isn't there something satisfying about turning your back on someone who has behaved badly? Something powerful about cutting that person out of your life? Something comforting about knowing that he or she is really to blame for what's wrong with your life? The truth is, no matter how good these emotions feel in the moment, they cannot and do not bring true or lasting happiness.

Harboring a grudge completely blocks our ability to have peace of mind. All sorts of studies indicate that negative thoughts, feelings, words, and behaviors affect our mental and physical health, our success, and our self-worth. An unwillingness to forgive is like stabbing ourselves with a knife and expecting the person who did us wrong to feel the pain. Forgiveness is not something we do for the sake of another person. Forgiveness is something we do for ourselves.

Think of forgiveness as emotional housecleaning. It lets

us make room for the good we desire. It also lets us go as far as we can on this spiritual journey and receive all the universe has to offer. If we refuse to forgive, we are clinging to self-defeating feelings such as guilt, shame, blame, hurt, and resentment, and when we do this, we cannot feel truly worthy of having the best God can give us; we cannot—and will not—accept God's gifts.

Many folks find practicing forgiveness almost as difficult as tithing. Some folks might even find it more difficult. But we have to do it, and no one is exempt. It was one of Jesus' main teachings, after all, and he was very clear about what he wanted us to do.

CHRIST AND FORGIVENESS

My belief is that Jesus came to this planet to teach us some remarkable things. He came to teach us how to master materiality. He wanted to teach us how to turn water into wine, to manifest divinity with whatever was at hand, to heal the sick with a word, a touch, a little mud and spit.

But when Jesus got here and saw what he had to work with, he revised his plans and began with the most basic of teachings, the kindergarten teachings, the Dick and Jane teachings, if you will. Over and over, Jesus stressed his most fundamental edicts—that we must love one another and that we must forgive one another.

Have we made any progress in these areas since he last paid us a visit? Hardly. It's been two thousand years, and yet here we are still saying, "We don't want to forgive. It is *their* fault; they are to blame." Sometimes I think if Jesus came back now he would just thump us for being so pigheaded. Just thump us!

We have to learn how to let go of long-harbored resentments and finally just forgive. We have to forgive our ex-spouses who didn't live up to our expectations. (How annoying it was of them to not be who we wanted them to be!) We have to forgive our children. We have to forgive our parents, especially. We have to come to realize that our parents loved us the best possible way they knew how. (You know, your parents had only one job—to get you safely onto the planet. If they managed that for you, anything more was gravy.) And, as with tithing, we must learn to forgive freely, joyfully, and completely.

JUDGING OTHER PEOPLE

When you have a problem with someone, it's almost always because they are not behaving the way that you want them to behave. Well, they are going to behave the way that they are going to behave, no matter what you think. Once you accept that, and love them just the way they are without judgment (as God does), then you will have achieved forgiveness.

I believe that understanding this truth is a lifelong process. And judging others is such a temptation that sometimes, even late in life, we are still doing it. I certainly saw that happen in my own family. For example, when I was a teenager (and just beginning to learn enough about metaphysics to be dangerous), my sweet little grandmother was living with us. Every evening she would sit in front of the TV in her rocking chair with her snuff and her spittoon.

At the time, the police in Houston were trying to have a big campaign against the "ladies of the evening," and they tried to embarrass those ladies by filming them being hand-cuffed and fingerprinted. And every night my granny would sit with her snuff, rocking in her rocking chair and spitting into her spittoon, and watching those women being locked up in jail.

Every evening, my grandmother would say the same thing. "Those hussies!" she'd say. "I hope they hang 'em."

Eventually, I got tired of hearing that. So one day I asked her, "Granny, do you know what reincarnation is?"

"No," she said. "What's that?"

"Some people believe that what you condemn in this life, you condemn yourself to experience in the next."

When she understood what I was saying, my granny's eyes got as big as saucers.

> "Do what you feel in your heart to be right, for you'll be criticized anyway. You'll be damned if you do and damned if you don't."
>
> —Eleanor Roosevelt

The next evening my grand-mother sat down in her rocking chair with her snuff and turned on the evening news. Once again, they played footage of women of ill repute being ar-rested and locked up. I was watching my granny to see what she would do or say. Finally, she took a deep breath.

"Well, *bless their hearts*," she said.

And that's the best thing we can do—to simply say, "Well, bless their hearts." We must not stand in judgment of other people, and we must not lay blame on them for doing what they do. Instead, we must recognize that what they are doing or not doing is simply none of our business.

I love that Scripture that says, "There is now no condemnation within me." As my other granny used to say, "Honey, there ain't no rocks in my pocket." Don't be throwing stones at anyone.

LEARNING TO LIVE WITHOUT LAYING BLAME

"Judge not" is a powerful admonition that we tend to ignore. Not only do we judge our friends and neighbors, but we judge and blame people we don't even know. Every few years, a high-profile murder or celebrity trial comes up, and everyone is abuzz with opinion. "He's guilty," we say or, "I just know she did it." The entire nation grinds to a halt when it's time for the verdict. But the truth is it's none of our business what another person did or did not do. If you're not directly involved in a situation, just stay out of it. As Jesus said, "Why beholdest thou the mote that is in thy brother's eye, but considerest not the beam that is in thine own eye?" Meaning that you have too much work in front of you to take the big wooden log out of your own eye to be worrying about the tiny speck of wood in someone else's.

Part of our problem is that laying blame is a cultural norm in today's world. We live in a society where we are constantly slapping each other with lawsuits. Anyone who watches the news will agree that whenever there is a story about something that's gone wrong, one of the first goals of the media is to find out whose fault it is, who's to blame, who's responsible for the mess.

But I believe that on our spiritual path, we must learn to ask new questions. Instead of asking, "Who's to blame?" we should instead ask, "How can we solve this, fix this, make this better?"

Humans are problem-solving critters. It's our nature to find answers, seek solutions, fix what's broken. But simple forgiveness is the best possible tool for "fixing what's broken" in our bodies, in our relationships, in our finances, in our careers, and in our world. Forgiveness frees us from the endless loop of blame and bad feeling that keeps our minds focused on all the wrong things. With forgiveness, we can let go of the past and turn to other, more important issues in our lives—such as how to be truly happy, to have the things we want, and to thrive with a sense that we are joyfully fulfilling our life purpose.

My optimism tells me that our earthly family is on the verge of an enormous spiritual breakthrough where simple forgiveness will be the order of the day and we will no longer ask, "Who can I blame?" but rather, "How can I serve?"

TO WHAT EXTENT DO WE FORGIVE?

On our spiritual journey toward prosperity, we are aspiring to a forgiveness that's so deep, full, and complete that no traces of any bad feeling at all will remain within us. This is a drastic kind of forgiveness that many of us have never experienced before. It may at first seem impossible to achieve, especially for those of us who have harbored grudges for ten, twenty, thirty years or more. But it's not.

Many people commonly believe they should aspire to the "Do unto others" rule when it comes to forgiveness. For example, in the Lord's Prayer, we ask that God "forgive us our trespasses as we forgive those who trespass against us." This is certainly a good and powerful statement, but I ask, do we really want to be forgiven in the manner and to the same degree that we forgive others?

I don't think so. I think we want to be forgiven in a deeper way . . . because in truth, many of us are not yet forgiving the other people in our lives deeply and completely. We might have talked about the concept and praised it, but then not actually done it. We might still harbor blame, judgment, condemnation, guilt, resentment, and shame. In this case then, until we learn to practice complete forgiveness, we want to be *more* forgiven than we forgive others.

If we truly want to forgive others completely (so that we ourselves may be forgiven completely), then we need to get busy cleaning our inner psyches. We can begin by asking ourselves prayerfully:

1. Whom am I blaming?
2. What am I blaming this person for?
3. Why am I blaming this person?
4. Who hurt me?
5. Why did I allow this person to hurt me?

6. What do I need to forgive, in myself, in my parents, in the government, and in my world?
7. Whom have I hurt?
8. Why did I hurt this person?
9. In what ways do I punish myself and others?

THE ROLE WE OURSELVES PLAY

One giant step toward emotional health is to realize that no one can hurt us unless we allow them to hurt us. In reality, no one can do to us what we are not already doing to ourselves. Let's say, for example, that you are feeling hurt, or sad, or disappointed because someone betrayed you. It's much easier to blame someone or something than it is to ask sincerely in prayer, "How am I betraying myself?" In other words:

- No one can steal from you unless you are a thief.
- No one can cheat you unless you are a cheater.
- No one can gossip about you unless you are a gossip.

At first, these ideas were very difficult for me to accept. For example, many years ago, my jewelry was stolen, and I was furious. This was not supposed to happen to me. I was a spiritual teacher on a spiritual path, teaching and serving. I was indignant and getting ready to give God a real piece of my mind. So I went to my spiritual teacher, ranting and raving about how unfair it was that something of mine had been stolen.

My teacher declared, "No one can steal from you unless you steal."

This made me so angry that smoke started coming out of my ears. "I do not steal!" I shouted at her.

"Oh, yes you do," she responded. "You are stealing my time right now."

What a wake-up call that moment was for me, and I then began a whole new process of understanding the importance of forgiveness and how I can achieve it.

When I first heard that old saying, "If you see a flaw in another person, it's your vision that needs correction," I did not believe it was true. The older I get and the more I forgive, however, the more I see that it is a powerful truth for my life.

REFRAMING THE STORY

The brand of true forgiveness I'm talking about in this chapter can be difficult to swallow when you think about the truly terrible things that people do to each other. For example, you might ask, "What about the sexual abuse of a child? How can a person be asked to forgive something as terrible as that?" And it is true that people do enormously dreadful things to other people. I myself was a victim of childhood sexual abuse, so I know full well the devastation that kind of betrayal can cause in a person's life. From the time I was four months old until I was four years old, I was sexually abused so badly that it almost killed me.

Let's be honest. If someone hurts you or betrays you in a truly terrible way, it's often difficult to forgive that person. In fact, it is probably the most difficult thing that you can do, especially if

- You were done wrong
- You were treated cruelly
- You were lied to
- You were stolen from
- You were abandoned
- You were molested
- You were raped
- You were cheated on
- You were battered
- You were betrayed

I'm sure you can see where I'm going with this. It's so easy to blame the other person—and so comforting to take on the role of the injured innocent. In regard to my own experience with sexual abuse, I had a particularly difficult time dealing with the effect it had on my self-esteem, and for many years I played the victim.

I will be eternally grateful for a teacher who one day abruptly called me on my act. As I once again began my tale of woe, he said, "Listen, Toots, this victim stuff has gone far enough. It's really a drag, and it's boring the tears out of the rest of us."

I was shocked; he had not given me the "poor baby" response that I had come to expect. As I gasped, he continued, "In order to heal this childhood trauma, what you've got to do is create a new story about it." He paused and gave it some thought.

"Okay. Here's your new story. Try this one on and see if it works for you. You came onto this planet to be a woman of power. Your soul chose this pathway, and because you chose it, you also chose to take an initiation in the misuse of power at a very young age. During this initiation you learned what it feels like when power is misused, and it is horrible. Therefore, it is now safe for you to be a woman of power in the world because you know now that you would never misuse nor abuse this power. And in this process, you have gained the most valuable of all spiritual gifts—the understanding heart."

My world reeled from this and cracked open a bit. It didn't happen overnight, but little by little, one day at a time, I began to embrace this wonderful new story, a saga that completely reordered my personal history. It made me feel powerful rather than helpless, and it allowed me to give up the role of victim.

It also brought to mind the coaching of another teacher who told me, "Never ask a 'why' question. There are no absolute answers to why questions. But if you absolutely have to ask why, at least have the good sense to make up an answer that pleases you." Lights began to come on in my mind and sparkle as I experienced another huge "Aha!" moment.

Now sometimes, when I discuss these issues, people ask, "If we are responsible for what happens to us, were you responsible for being sexually abused as a child?" The honest answer is that I don't know. I suppose some people might say that small children are exempt from some of life's laws. Others, if they believe in reincarnation, might believe it was the result of something done in a past lifetime. I don't know the answer to that question. I do know, however, that reframing the abuse has helped me achieve peace of mind, and that is a joy.

Our thoughts have a force of their own. In fact, the further we go on our spiritual journey, the more we come to understand that actually, every thought we have is a kind of prayer. And because prayer is so powerful, so are the thoughts that we have.

Catherine Ponder has a deep understanding of this power of thought. As she writes in her book *The Millionaire Joshua*, "The world you live in is the exact record of your thoughts. If you do not like the world you live in, then you do not like your thoughts. An uplifted mind is a magnet for all good things of the universe to hasten to you. Whereas, a depressed, anxious, critical, resentful state of mind becomes a magnet for trouble to fly to you. The choice is up to you."

With this in mind, we naturally see the importance of letting go of blame and judgment and other negative thoughts, and instead we turn to positive thoughts such as forgiveness so that we may manifest what we want in our lives. As I became more keenly aware of the truth of this, I eventually realized that I was going to have to develop a daily discipline to monitor my every thought, and that is a conscious discipline I practice to this day.

MY STORY OF FORGIVENESS

I want to share with you a little bit of my own personal soap opera. I'll admit it; I have created some drama in my life. In fact, I've created so much drama I've made *Days of Our Lives* look like child's play.

When I went overseas to teach school, back in my early twenties, I chose to go to Guam in the west Pacific. On my first day on the island, I met a gorgeous man. He was six-foot-four, with thick black curly hair, bright blue eyes, and the body of a god. He was also the chairman of the English Department, so I knew he had brains (not that that really mattered once I'd seen that gorgeous body!). God love him, when I showed up the poor man didn't stand a chance. I just snapped him up and married him right off the bat!

One of the reasons I'd chosen to go to Guam in the first place was that at the end of your two-year contract, the government of Guam would give you a trip around the world. Well, at the end of those two years, my new husband and I got ready to go on our trip.

As it so happened, I was six months pregnant. I was delighted to be expecting—I felt like an Earth mother—and I couldn't wait to meet my baby. I was never sick a day. Life was perfect. I had married Prince Charming, and now we were off to travel the world.

We started in Manila, in the Philippines, where we saw the famous rice terraces. From there we went to Tokyo and saw the Golden Buddha. Then we went to Hong Kong and rode the ferry across the harbor at sunset. All during the trip we did some serious shopping. We were just two peas in a pod, with a third on the way, and I was in heaven.

One day in Hong Kong, I got tuckered out from all the walking. I told my husband that I was going to go back to the hotel and take a nap. He wanted to keep sightseeing,

so we decided to meet back at the hotel and have dinner together. We kissed and went our separate ways.

I went back to the hotel and took a nice long nap. Then
I got dressed up and put on my jewelry and makeup, all
ready to go out. At around sunset, my husband came back
to the hotel room.

"Edwene, I don't love you anymore," he told me. "I'm
leaving."

I wish I could tell you that what I did was say, "Oh,
well, that's okay. Life is unfolding in a wonderful and harmonious way." But that's not exactly what I did. Instead, I
said some of the worst things to him that I've ever said
to anyone.

I lived the next seven years of my life in a state of complete rage. And if you've ever been there, you know it's a terrible place to live. I was angry at the whole world. Life was
unfair, people were rotten, and men, especially, were completely untrustworthy.

I became mean and bitter and ugly and sick. Only when
I came very close to dying of cancer did I finally understand
that I had to forgive this man. Because it was that, or give up
my own life. The problem was that I didn't know how to
start. The Bible tells us over and over and over that we have
to forgive, but it doesn't explain how.

So, I began working with an affirmation that went something like this: "I forgive you, you sorry son of a b----!"

I didn't really mean it when I said I forgave him, but
I said it anyway. And then the more I said it, the gentler I
became with it. I began to wonder, "What would cause

somebody to do something so terrible and heartless as he did to me?" I began to try to understand him and figure out where he was coming from—not because I was some great humanitarian, but because I understood that if I couldn't start to see things from his point of view I would never be able to let it go and start to truly live again.

Over the years, little by little, as I learned the forgiveness process, I began to feel compassion for him. I didn't want to have compassion for him! But I began to feel compassion and understanding, and over time I even began to feel some love for him again. Eventually I came to realize that what he did was the only possible option for him at the time. He had come from a family with twelve children that had really struggled, and I think the idea of having a child just scared him to death. I believe the feelings of fear and the need to flee were just too powerful for him to overcome in that moment.

> "How do the geese know when to fly to the sun? Who tells them the seasons? How do we, humans, know when it is time to move on? As with the migrant birds, so surely with us, there is a voice within, if only we would listen to it, that tells us so certainly when to go forth into the unknown."
>
> —Elisabeth Kübler-Ross

I can say now without one doubt that I have completely and totally forgiven him, which is reflected in the wonderful relationship that he and I now have. These days, every time I go to Washington, D.C., where he lives, I have dinner with him and his lovely wife. The two of them have become very dear friends of mine, and the three of us even attended my daughter's graduation together. I was so pleased to be able to sit with my former husband and his new wife as a family, and then for the four of us to attend a graduation party afterwards and really be together to help my daughter celebrate her accomplishment.

Of course, none of this happened overnight. But it did happen eventually, and from the experience I learned the following fundamental truth about forgiveness: The people who do us wrong are our teachers. From them we can learn invaluable spiritual lessons about compassion and understanding. At the time, what he did to me seemed like one of the worst things that anyone has ever done to me. But today I am so thankful for what happened in that hotel room in Hong Kong, because without it I might never have learned the life-transforming power of true forgiveness.

Now, so that I am clear, when I say you must forgive people, I don't mean that you need to endlessly put up with bad behavior. You are permitted to stand up for yourself and what you believe to be right. So if people have hurt or mistreated you in the past, and you suspect that they would do it again in the future given the chance, there is no law that says you have to keep them in your life. You do, however, have to forgive them for what they did.

It cannot be stated enough that forgiveness can be very difficult. If you find yourself trying to forgive someone, yet still feel resentment despite your best efforts, don't despair. Just pray for help and keep trying. What is important is not that you achieve a perfect and saintly life in which you never, ever feel a bad feeling toward another person. What *is* important is that you make the very best effort that you can.

FORGIVENESS AND FINANCIAL DEBT

Forgiveness is a wonderful gift that will help you achieve greater serenity and peace of mind. But the rewards you get from it are not just emotional; they are financial, too. For example, some of you reading this book may be in debt. Well, you're not going to get out of that debt until you learn how to forgive. It's okay to consider transferring balances to a credit card with a lower interest rate or mortgaging your home. However, if there is any debt in your life and you want to get out of debt, the quickest way to do so is to forgive.

Let me give you an example from my own life. My former husband, when he walked out on me, left me with $60,000 worth of debt on credit cards in my name that I did not know existed. After I overcame my shock and fury that I was now $60,000 in debt, and once I had stewed about it for a couple of days, I realized that being angry was not going to get me out of this crisis.

The first thing I did was to acknowledge the role I had played in the situation. The credit cards were in my name, and the reason I did not know about them was that I had not paid attention to all the bills that were arriving in the mail. Since I had let him pay them while I went on my merry way, I had to acknowledge that I was partly responsible for the mess I now found myself in.

Up to that point I had a wonderful credit rating, and I wanted to keep it that way, so I decided to take responsibility for those debts. I asked God to please help me repay them, and I trusted that with God's help I would find a way to pay the credit cards off. (I could have made my ex pay them, and my attorney certainly wanted me to, but I knew that would keep the battle going on between us, and I did not want my life to be consumed by being at war with this man.)

One day around that time, I was clearing out the basement, and I found a box with some of my ex-husband's things in it. And one of those things was a journal.

Well, I gave into temptation and read that journal, and I'm very sorry that I did because he wrote some very nasty and cruel things about me in it. They were written during a time that he was buying me jewelry and sending me flowers, and during a time that I really believed he loved me. I thought what he wrote was unkind and unfair, and his words wounded me deeply.

It was really devastating, and I did not want to feel that level of pain. I said to myself, "This will not do."

So I took the journal and held a ceremony. I burned the journal, and at the same time I made affirmative prayer statements for his good and blessed him. I thanked God for making him my teacher, and for forcing me to stand in my own truth and strength and integrity.

In other words, I forgave him. I forgave him for leaving me with a debt, and I forgave him for his unkind words, too.

Now as it so happened, for several years previously I had been working with a couple who wanted to sell their business. They would call me every month, we would pray together and do visualization. Well, the very next week after I had my forgiveness ceremony, the couple called me and said, "We've sold the business," and they sent me a tithe for $20,000. Getting that tithe was the concrete beginning of my being able to forgive my way out of that debt, and in three months I was able to completely pay off the credit cards. While I hope never to be in debt again in my life, if I find myself in that unfortunate position I will sit down and do another careful self-examination to see if there is anyone that I am not forgiving.

(On the subject of debt, let me be clear about one thing. There is a distinction between unsecured financial debt—say, when you're racking up debt on a credit card with no idea how you'll pay it back—and what I've heard called "the wise use of credit," such as having a mortgage on a home or taking a student loan so that you can get a good education. If you're wondering what kind of debt you're getting into, turn inward. If the debt feels burdensome, it might be due to unwise spending. But if it gives you a sense of security or greater potential for your future, it may well simply be "the wise use of credit.")

Forgiveness is an act of will: You make yourself do it. You don't do it because it feels good, or because you want to do it. You do it because the Master told you to do it.

Like many of the other laws in this book, practicing true forgiveness is not easy. As is often the case when we make changes in life, we may need to be very patient with ourselves while we learn to practice this new habit. It's okay to practice it imperfectly. But do practice it, because forgiveness will change your life.

Give yourself the gift of forgiveness so that you, too, may know the great joy that is the result of living without judgment or blame.

CHAPTER 7

MAKING FORGIVENESS A DAILY PRACTICE

It's completely normal to feel resistance when you start doing forgiveness work, especially when someone has done something truly terrible that has had disastrous effects throughout your life. Looking back on what that person did, you might be inclined to say, "I have a right to my anger. Bad things have happened because of this person." And a case could be made for that position; perhaps you do have a right to your anger. You also have a right to take a screwdriver and stick it into an electrical outlet. But whom would you hurt by doing so? Keep in mind, we don't practice forgiveness for the benefit of the other guy. *We do it for ourselves.*

If everyone on Earth were to practice forgiveness as a daily discipline, life on this planet would be completely transformed. And that planetary transformation can start today, with you and me.

So how do we begin? What is the process? Allow me to share five simple forgiveness techniques that can transform your life and your world. Try each one and see which work for you. You might want to use a combination of them, or after having tried them all, you might want to invent some of your own.

FORGIVENESS TECHNIQUE NUMBER 1

Writing, speaking, and listening to forgiveness affirmations are all effective ways to begin the process of forgiveness. You can use some of those below, or you can make up your own. The key to creating powerful, transforming affirmations is to say what you want to be true as if it is already true. Here are some that I use:

- I forgive myself completely for every mistake I have ever made.
- I forgive others, knowing that we all did the best we could at that time.
- I let go of guilt, blame, shame, judgment, and hurt.
- I am free from condemnation.
- I forgive my parents completely.
- I forgive everyone who did not give me the love and attention I desired.
- I forgive myself for my unconscious behaviors of the past, and I forgive others theirs as well.
- I allow myself to feel forgiven and to move forward in life.

FORGIVENESS TECHNIQUE NUMBER 2

Every night before I go to sleep, I ask myself prayerfully, "Have I put anyone outside my heart today?" I am not proud to say that usually I have, and it's always for the same reason: Some poor soul did not get Queen Edwene's edict about how to behave on planet Earth.

Then I take time to forgive myself for this judgment made in an unconscious moment, and to release my need to control others' behavior. I come once again to the realization that how others act, drive, dress, speak, spend, vote, and generally behave is *none of my business*. As my daddy used to remind me, "Edwene, just tend to your own rat killing!"

What I have noticed about my own forgiveness process is that the only people I ever have to forgive are those people who do not do things my way. And there are a lot of them. And many of them drive automobiles.

So I take some time each evening, inviting them back into my heart space, looking to see what caused me to toss them out, forgiving them and myself, and making a new commitment to be more awake and aware.

FORGIVENESS TECHNIQUE NUMBER 3

At least once a year, but usually more often, I do a complete forgiveness inventory of my entire life. I set aside a day and find a quiet place to face myself and my past. Alone and uninterrupted, I mentally go through my whole life as far back as I can remember, double-checking my feelings and memories to see if I've overlooked or forgotten or neglected to forgive someone. I review my early childhood—my parents, friends, family members, classmates, teachers—and then I go up through the teenage years, then to college, and then to bosses, work colleagues, etc., etc. If I am doing the exercise properly, it can take quite a while.

> "Don't compromise yourself. You are all you've got."
>
> —Janis Joplin

Several years ago while taking my own inventory, when I recalled an experience with my ex-husband who had struggled with substance abuse, I had some unexpected negative feelings. I felt hurt, blame, and judgment as I remembered old feelings of betrayal and humiliation. It felt terrible to me to re-experience this, and I was ashamed at my lack of forgiveness. I thought that I had forgiven us both for everything.

I then knew that I had some work to do. I began with earnestness to change my feelings by praying and affirming good for him. I began to speak aloud positive statements about him, as a form of prayer treatment.

"I see you happy, healthy, and whole, completely forgiven for all mistakes of the past.

"I see you successful and prosperous, creative, making a contribution to your world.

"I see you in satisfying relationships, enjoying your life, supported and nurtured in every way.

"I see you in a wonderful home, traveling, beautifully clothed, driving a magnificent car, doing all you've ever dreamed of doing.

"I see you peaceful and joyous in all ways." And so on.

I had not seen this man in many years and didn't know where he was or what he was doing, so I was astonished to receive a letter from him the very next week. He had tracked me down, found my address, and had taken the time to write me a precious and priceless letter:

Dear Edwene,

You have been on my mind a lot lately. I wanted to touch base with you to let you know how wonderful my life is these days. My business is now extremely successful. I am happily married, and we have a beautiful new home. My kids have graduated from college and are doing well. We get to travel a lot. Our health is good and life is sweet.

I'm writing you this note because I want to thank you for the contributions you have made to my life. I remember with joy the fun times we had and the laughter we shared and I recall with bittersweet poignancy some of the difficult lessons we had to learn together.

My point here is to let you know that however sweet my life is now, I know that your life must be even better.

I was so touched and grateful for this letter. He also included a check for $3,000 to make good on a debt I had given up on long before.

Needless to say, I now pray for this man every week!

FORGIVENESS TECHNIQUE NUMBER 4

Perhaps the person you need to forgive is yourself. Say you did some things in the past that you know were wrong, and you never apologized or made amends, so now you feel guilty. You haven't been forgiven by others, and you haven't been forgiven by your own self.

Every dog has a few fleas; we've all done bad things at one time or another. I know I have, and I wouldn't want some of those things listed on the blimp going over the Super Bowl. I wouldn't want my granny to know some of the things I've done. But sharing with at least one other person is vitally important to your peace of mind.

Many years ago, because of my then-husband's substance abuse, I started going to Al-Anon so that I could fix him and make him become the person I wanted him to be. And one of the exercises in Al-Anon is that you have to take a fearless and searching inventory of your errors and your failings. You must go back over your life and write down every single dumb or wrong thing you have ever done. (For some of us, this will take a while.) Then you must share your list with someone else. Catholics calls this "confession." But we can all do it.

Of course, you don't go out and confess to the whole world. Find someone you trust, explain what you want to do, and ask this person to be there for you. Choose that person with care. Make sure he or she will honor you and never tell your secrets or try to shame you. And then you must share your list of wrongdoings with that person, leaving out nothing.

This confidante doesn't have to comment about any of it. He or she is simply a silent, impartial listener. There is no burden on him or her to absolve you of what you've done; that's not the confidante's role. All he or she has to do is sit and listen to you without judgment. But even though that's all this person has to do, the healing that can result from it is extraordinary. Just the telling of something can release it.

Well, I was terrified. I had never told anyone anything that I had done wrong. But I wanted to fix my husband so badly that I followed all of Al-Anon's directions. I myself chose a woman I knew well and trusted, and I sat down with her. Very fearfully, I admitted to her every single thing I had ever done wrong in my life. When I was done with my list I was horrified, wondering what she would say or if she would even be willing to speak to me anymore, now that she knew all these awful things about me. But when I was all done, she just smiled.

> "Fear is a question: What are you afraid of, and why? Just as the seed of health is in illness, because illness contains information, our fears are a treasure house of self-knowledge if we explore them."
>
> —Marilyn Ferguson

"That it?" she asked. "Honey, I've had worse things than that in my *eye*!"

FORGIVENESS TECHNIQUE NUMBER 5

Let's say you're feeling so bad about something that someone else did to you—or that you did to someone else—that you just can't take it. What do you do? You ask God for help. Because maybe you can't take it, but God can.

Imagine the person that for you is the holiest embodiment of God's love. Perhaps that person is Jesus Christ. Or Buddha. Or Mary. Or Mohammed. Or Quan Yin. Or the Dalai Lama. It doesn't matter who—just that this is a person whom you love and with whom you could speak to with total honesty and trust. (For this exercise, I will use Jesus.)

Find a quiet place where you won't be disturbed, sit in a comfortable position, and close your eyes. Take a deep breath and relax your body. Imagine that Jesus is right there with you, right beside you, holding your hand, and with one arm around you. He is saying, "I love you. I love you with an everlasting love. I've always loved you. There's nothing you've ever done or ever could do that would stop me from loving you."

Now feel that love. Feel your heart open up to receive that love. Feel it cleaning out all of the bad feelings of guilt and blame inside you.

Next, call to mind anyone that you need to forgive but who you haven't been able to. What you can't do, Jesus

Christ can. Imagine that person right there with you and Jesus. Tell that person whatever you need to tell them to forgive them. Feel that healing taking place. And if anyone else comes to mind, bring them up so that you and Jesus can forgive them, too.

Now, bring up anything bad that you've done that you feel guilty about. You don't have to tell Jesus about it. He already knows all about it and loves you anyway. But you may need to ask for forgiveness, and for help in forgiving yourself. Ask for it, and then imagine Jesus smiling at you, saying, "My beloved, it's gone! You're free! You're not guilty!" Feel how wonderful it feels to let go of all that pain and guilt. You don't need those bad feelings anymore. Release them and let them go. Take a deep breath and say to yourself, "I'm free! I'm forgiven. I'm a new creature in Christ!"

This powerful exercise can help you achieve divine completion because once you have accepted forgiveness, it's done. You don't have to keep carrying around the guilt year after year, apologizing again and again, whipping yourself on the back and continuing to feel bad about what you did. You learn your lesson, forgive yourself, and then it's done.

That's a wonderful phrase: It is done. Do this exercise and then give yourself the great gift of saying, "It is done."

THE UNDERSTANDING HEART

I love the wonderful Old Testament story about when wise King Solomon was in prayer and God came to him and asked, "Solomon, what do you want?"

Now, metaphysically, Solomon represents that wisdom faculty within you and within me that is always in prayer, and that is always acknowledging and beholding God as the beloved presence within. And that presence in us is always saying, "What do you want?"

What do you want? All we ever have to do is respond to that question. The universe is asking you every day, "What do you want?" And most of humanity, instead of answering it, is instead focused on, "Look at what that person did to me," and "Poor me," and "Isn't life awful?"

Forgiveness is about shifting out of our human tendency to wallow in a victim state so that our minds are clear enough to come to realize: Oh my God, we can have what we want!

Solomon ponders the question. You can tell in the Scripture he's really wondering what a good answer would be. He knows that he has a people and a nation to rule, and in his mind his subjects are kind of unruly and don't follow instructions. (Kind of like how we are, with all our negative thoughts and feelings, right?) And Solomon says, in effect, "You know, God, I have to rule this nation, to handle and to take care of this people. Give therefore thy servant an understanding heart."

And we are told in Scripture that this answer pleased God. And God said, "Because you have not asked for riches, nor have you asked for honor, but you have instead asked for an understanding heart, not only will I give you that, but I will give you riches and honor, as well." (1 Kings 3:11–13)

What it means to have an understanding heart is that you can't blame anybody for anything. You can't blame your ex-spouse, the Pope, the Internal Revenue Service, your boss, your hairdresser, the Republican Party, the Democratic Party, your parents, the Queen of England—anybody. And you especially cannot blame yourself. You have to live in a constant state of being forgiven. Would that be all right with you? Do you think you can forgo the sweet pain of punishing yourself endlessly? And do you think that if you're not constantly judging and blaming others, you and your friends will be able to find other things to talk about?

To have an understanding heart you must strive to live a life without blame, and the temptation to lay blame is a challenge you must face almost daily. Everywhere you go—whether to work, to church, or to the produce department of your local grocery store—there is bound to eventually be someone who will not recognize your absolute 100 percent magnificence and who is going to come up and say something that is going to annoy you. Well, take a deep breath and get over it. Don't go running around asking everyone, "Did you hear what she said?" Instead, say to yourself, "Hmm. How curious," and then move on.

Very gently and very lovingly, we've got to open our hearts so that there is truly no condemnation in us. Even toward the people who do truly bad things—we must strive to feel no disapproval. You can get on a train ride of condemnation, finding fault and assigning blame, but you don't want to be on that train. Because riding that train will make you sick, and you don't want to be sick. You want to be well.

I truly believe that no matter what terrible things other people have done to you in your lifetime, the unending dark night of the soul is optional. It's not part of the path you want to be on. Maybe you're getting some kind of payoff from wallowing in your suffering, and a lot of people are saying, "There, there, there, Baby," and then running away from you as quickly as they can, as they did when I was playing the victim. But being full of blame and self-pity is not the state for which you were created.

What is the state for which you were created? To be God's Beloved. To be cherished and adored by your heavenly Mother-Father as the wonderful and loveable being that you are. And the great love that God has for you is bigger than all the bad things you've ever done in your life and all the bad things that have been done to you.

There really is such a thing as true and total forgiveness, and the only person who has to do that forgiveness work is you, because God has never held anything against you. God doesn't see your sin. God doesn't see your faults. God just sees the bright, shining light that you really are, and God is saying to you all the time, "Honey, what can I do for you now?" It's God's good pleasure to give you the kingdom.

FORGIVENESS: A JOURNALING EXERCISE

When we've carried a grudge (whether against ourselves or others) for many years, it can be hard to know how to start letting go. A good way to start is to write out exactly what it is you want to forgive. Seeing a statement of forgiveness clearly written out in black and white can be a powerful way to help you forgive when you haven't been able to before. Fill in the following blanks in your journal and see if that simple act doesn't help you start to release long-held grudges.

I am through feeling guilty about:

_____

I am over feeling sorry for myself about:

_____

I am no longer going to blame _____ for:

_____

I am finished with all sadness about:

_____

I forgive my parents for:

_____

I release all suffering about:

_____

Above all, I forgive myself once and for all for:

_____

It is done!

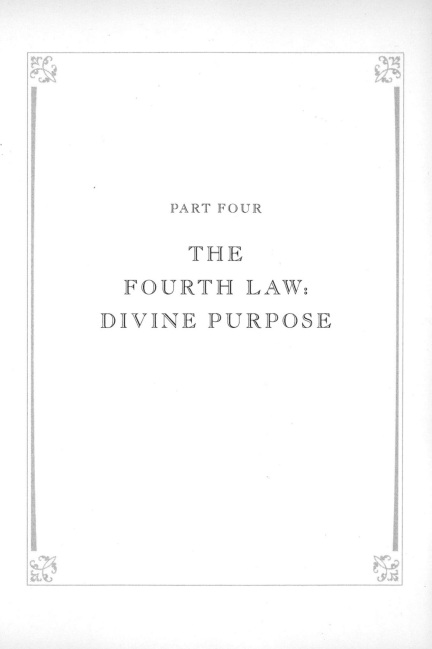

PART FOUR

THE
FOURTH LAW:
DIVINE PURPOSE

CHAPTER 8

THE IMPORTANCE OF COMMITMENT

You've been doing hard work in your journey toward prosperity—of which you should be very proud. What you will discover, if you haven't already, is that commitment plays a crucial role in each aspect of that journey. It takes commitment to tithe not just every once in a while, but each and every time money comes into your life. It takes commitment to set goals and then to move outside your comfort zones in order to achieve them. It certainly takes great commitment to forgive the people who have hurt you in the past. And as you will discover as we move into our fourth law, it will take commitment to start living according to your divine purpose.

What I know with clarity and certainty is that when you make a 100 percent commitment to do or to be something, and you take every step with integrity, the universe will open up a way where before there was no way; the universe will rush in to support you. Now, when I use the word "commitment" I am not talking about a vague, hazy, wishy-washy comment like, "I'll do it if it seems like it will work out." I am talking about a passionate, 100 percent commitment—

where we say, "I'm going to do it, by God, come hell or high water!" When we have that level of commitment, we are completely unstoppable. Most people have no idea how much power they have. Well, if you want to exercise that power, you can do so through commitment.

Don't worry if you don't know how to do the thing you are committing to do. In 1976, when I made a commitment to the Lord of my being that I would be 100 percent responsible for the transformation of the abundance-consciousness of planet Earth, I didn't have the foggiest notion how to do it. But one of my teachers said to me, "Edwene, you didn't know how to do puberty, either!"

Consciously, I didn't know how to be born on this planet. Consciously, I did not know how to birth a child, and yet somehow I was able to do those wonderful things. And once I made a commitment to start helping people transform their lives completely, I have been able to do that, too.

One of my favorite quotations is "Courage is the commitment to begin, without any guarantee of success." Let's take as an example my story about rappelling down the cavern. I didn't have any guarantee that I would be successful in getting down the side of that cave without falling. But I made a commitment to begin. Now, once I made the commitment by stepping off the ledge, I couldn't go back up. The only way out was down. The only sure-fire way to know whether you've made a commitment is when there's no turning back and the only way out is through, all the way to the other side, because if there's a side way out of it, that's not a commitment. That is so important, I'm going to say it again: *If there's a way out, it's not a commitment.*

What should you commit to? As you know, my focus in this book is on prosperity. Because you have read this far, I imagine that you would be willing to make a commitment to prosper. Or maybe you want to go beyond that and commit to making a real change in the world.

Some of us have gone through hard times in the past and are here today simply because we made a commitment to survive. But we're here for much more than that. We should move beyond a commitment to survive into a commitment to prosper. Then, beyond that, we must make a commitment to make this a better world. That's why we're really here. You might want to start with a prosperity commitment, and then graduate to a commitment to doing good in the world in a real and concrete way.

The truth about you is that you are a spiritual being, living in a spiritual universe, governed by spiritual law. You came to this planet to play at the highest level that has ever been played. You came to play at the level of Gandhi, of Dr. Martin Luther King, of Mother Teresa, at the level of every great and wise soul who ever made a difference. You came to play with the big kids.

What problem do you feel passionately needs to be solved? Racism? Homelessness? Child abuse? You find your great spiritual commitments by following your passions, by seeking to identify the one thing that you really, really are committed to changing for all humanity. And one that might also be fun to do. Remember, no matter how lofty our spiritual goals, they must also be fun.

VERBALIZING YOUR COMMITMENT

There is extraordinary power in the spoken word. I believe that when you say something, it automatically takes on enormous strength. After all, we learn in the book of Genesis that God spoke the world into being. You, too, create your own world with words. You begin to bring your commitment into being simply by speaking.

Now, if your commitment is weak and you're feeling unsure, people will know it when you verbalize your commitment. The first time I verbalized my commitment to transform the way everyone on Earth thought about money and prosperity, I thought I was going to have to go and pick people up off the floor, they were laughing so hard. That's because I was still a little hesitant. When you verbalize a commitment, the response you get from the universe is going to directly mirror what you're feeling inside. Now that I have a much stronger sense of myself, my power, and my intention, the reaction I get is completely different.

Always keep this in mind: "A commitment verbalized automatically creates its own support team." Once you say your commitment aloud, with faith and conviction, you immediately draw to you those people, ideas, coincidences, and synchronicity of events that say to you, "Oh, yes! I'm here to help you with that commitment!" You draw your team to you.

In one commitment workshop I taught, there was a woman who decided she wanted to verbalize her commitment. She told me, "I've been working on this for five years, and I've not had any real breakthrough results. I think it's because I have never stated publicly what I'm doing. And I want to state it for this group."

So she mustered her courage, took a deep breath, and said, "I am 100 percent committed to creating a halfway house for children who have been on drugs and cannot go back into their home environments. I don't want them to have to go into Social Services. I want the halfway house to have spiritual principles, firm discipline, and guidelines to keep these young people there until they are recovered." She finished by saying, "I've found the location and what I need to get started is $13,000."

When the workshop was over, another participant approached her and said, "My son is one of those children. You go get the paperwork, and you tell me what you need, and I will see that you have it." Then he wrote out a check for $13,000.

She verbalized her commitment, and someone stepped up to join her support team.

You can have the same results.

Now, you don't know who or where your team members are. They may be nearby, but then again they may be in Mongolia. But once you say the word, you start moving them toward you. That's how powerful your spoken word is. Your spoken word goes to the ends of the universe and is returned to you—and it doesn't return to you empty. It comes back to you full to overflowing with that which you decree and declare.

God is waiting for you to speak your choices with faith and conviction and to see that you're in motion. God can't drive a parked car. It's no good saying, "I've got all these great ideas, and nothing's happening!" God is ready when you are. God is completely ready, on standby, just waiting for the signal that you're ready to go. And the signal is when you speak your commitment out loud and then take concrete action.

For so many years, I prayed, "God, this is Edwene. I'm right here. Just tell me what you want—anything—and I'll do it. Whatever you want, I'll be there. I'm right behind you, ready to go—just give me a sign."

Well, finally I got quiet enough, and I heard God. And what I heard was, "Edwene, this is God. I'm right here. Just tell me what you want—anything—and I'll do it. Whatever you want, I'll be there . . ."

MILDRED'S COMMITMENT STORY

The story of Mildred is one that I'm not sure I would have believed if I hadn't witnessed it myself. It's a story about a woman who taught me what a true prosperity commitment is really all about.

Back in the mid-eighties, it was all over the news that Halley's Comet—which only came over the Earth every 70 or so years—was soon going to appear in the sky, and I was fascinated by the notion. I was enthralled by the idea of seeing the comet, and since the newspapers reported that the best possible view of Halley's Comet was going to be in the South Pacific, I decided that I wanted to go to that part of the world. Unfortunately, I didn't know how I was going to manage it because I didn't have the money, but I knew that "how" was none of my business. I just had to ask for some assistance.

One night I went into prayer. I said, "Now look, God, you know that I really want to go to the South Pacific to see Halley's Comet, and you know that I don't have the money, but I'm not worried because I know you have everything handled. However, if there is anything I can do to help make it happen, please let me know. Please send me a divine idea."

Well, the next morning I woke up with a divine idea. I called a cruise company and said, "I want to have a Success Seminar at Sea where I take a group of people on a cruise to the South Pacific to see Halley's Comet. I would like you to have an astronomer on board with a telescope on the upper deck so that every evening we can look at the sky. And I think that if I sell enough places, I should get mine for free. How many berths would I have to sell in order to get a free one for myself?"

"Eighteen," said the man at the cruise company. "And if you can manage to do that, I'll put you in first class."

So, I put together a brochure for my Success Seminar at Sea and started to announce at my workshops that I was going to take this wonderful trip, and that I would love for others to come with me. We would start by flying to Tahiti and spending two nights in a luxury hotel, then board a beautiful French ship and spend seven nights in the South Pacific. Then, it was back to the Tahitian luxury hotel. The total cost was going to be $3,000, and if a person wanted to come along I needed a deposit of $1,000 to hold a space.

One day I was giving a workshop at a little church in the Midwest. After I'd talked about the trip, a little white-haired woman named Mildred came up to me, handed me a folded check, and said, "I'm going to go on the cruise with you. Here's my deposit."

"Wonderful," I said. "We're going to have a great time."

I set the check aside. Later that day, I looked at it to make sure she'd included a telephone number so that I could contact her. But when I looked at the check, I saw that it wasn't made out for $1,000. It was made out for $10.

Maybe I wasn't clear, I thought. I went and found Mildred.

"Please forgive me," I told her. "I don't think I communicated very clearly. In order to hold your space, I need a deposit of $1,000."

"Oh, I heard you, Honey." Mildred said. "I don't have $1,000 right now, but I'm going on that cruise. So keep my check."

I didn't want to rain on her parade, so I let it drop. Well, over the next few weeks, small checks from Mildred started drifting in. One came in for $3.95. Two or three days later, I got one for $4.50, and then I got one for $7.95, and then I got a really big one, for $12.50, and so on. By the deadline, when I had my 18 people enrolled, Mildred had given me about $97.

I really prayed about calling her. I wanted to break it to her very gently that she wouldn't be coming on the cruise. I wanted to make sure she was empowered and not diminished by the experience. So I called her, and I said, "Mildred, my trip is now full. So I'm going to return your $97, and I just know that the next time we have an opportunity to have an adventure together, that it's going to work out perfectly, and we'll have a great time."

"Oh, no you don't," said Mildred. "You keep my deposit. I'm going on that cruise!"

Well, at this point I began to wonder what I was dealing with. I was starting to think that Mildred might be a few sandwiches short of a full picnic. So I began to speak very slowly and clearly.

"I don't want to be rude, but I don't think you understand exactly what I'm saying," I told her. "I want to be real clear so that you understand me. The cost of the cruise is $3,000. What I would need from you is complete payment of $3,000, but at this point even that would be no good because the trip is full. I wouldn't have room for you anyway. So I'm going to return your $97. I'm really sorry."

She said, "Dearie-pie, I understand perfectly. The problem we're having here is not that I'm not understanding you; it's that *you're* not understanding *me*! I am going on that cruise."

Well, I didn't know what to do, so I took the coward's way out. Instead of arguing with her any more I just said, "Okay. We'll pray about it," and hung up. I thought I'd just send her the money back after I returned from the trip.

Packing and getting ready for my Seminar at Sea was a lot of work, and I kind of forgot about Mildred while I got ready for the trip. Then, two days before we were scheduled to depart, I got a call from a very wealthy woman in Birmingham, Alabama, who was one of the first people enrolled to go on the cruise.

"Edwene," she told me, "I'm in a real pickle. We have a family court case that's come up, and I simply *have* to be there. I've tried everything I can to get the judge to postpone it for one week so that I can go on the trip, but he won't do it. Now, I've gone on enough cruises in my life to know that it's much too late for me to get a refund. Do you know anyone who would like to go in my place?"

I could not believe what I was hearing. I could hardly wait to call Mildred and give her the news. I got her on the phone and said, "You're simply not going to believe what I am about to tell you!"

"Oh, there's no need to tell me, Honey!" she said. "My bags are already packed and waiting by the front door."

Charles Fillmore said that the quickest way to have your demonstration of good is to believe the promise of Jesus Christ, who says to you, "Whosoever shall not doubt in his heart, but shall believe that what he saith cometh to pass, he shall have it."

This is so important; look at this statement carefully: *Whosoever shall not doubt in her heart, but shall believe that what she saith cometh to pass, she shall have it.* Mildred never doubted for one moment that she was coming with me on the cruise. I certainly doubted it, but she didn't. She had made a complete and total commitment in her mind to go on the trip, and because she made her choice and then verbalized it, God stepped in and did exactly what was needed.

HOW THE PROCESS WORKS

Now, Mildred's is a great story, and it's one I enjoy sharing because it illustrates so beautifully the power of verbalization, but verbalization isn't all there is to the commitment process. It's only one step. Once we have made our commitment, and verbalized it, we must then remain open to the signals that the universe may send back to us. One of several things may happen, which will let you know how to proceed.

You may get a "go" signal, which lets you know you're headed in the right direction. Then again, you may get a "stop" signal, which means that maybe you should step back and reassess your commitment. Thirdly, you may get what looks and seems like a "stop" signal but is actually something quite different, and which you should not allow to derail you. Let's look at those three different possibilities, one by one.

GETTING THE "GO" SIGNAL

If you have verbalized your commitment but aren't sure about what step to take next, ask for a "go" signal. I'm someone who doesn't mind asking God for a clear sign if I'm trying to make a decision. I guess some people think we shouldn't need that kind of guidance, or that we should be working on a higher plane when it comes to making our decisions, but I'm an ardent believer that you will get what you ask for. And if you ask for guidance, you'll get it.

A "go" signal can take different forms. Sometimes we get an outside sign, like a physical object or occurrence that makes us feel we've been sent a message. Or maybe the sign will come from inside. I believe that we all have an internal guidance system—our intuition, if you will—that can tell us what to do, if only we're willing to stop and listen. It's the little voice inside us, the voice of God, telling us when we're on the right track. I call it the "go" signal, when I get a clear sense of "This feels right; this is the right thing for me to do."

Around the time that I was being ordained, I didn't know where I was going to serve as a minister. I made a commitment that, in this matter, I would follow the will of God. I made the commitment that when it came to what I could do next, where I would serve, I would follow God's will as I understood it and experienced it with my indwelling guidance system—that little voice inside that always tells me the truth.

I had a lot of exciting possibilities being offered to me. For example, I had an invitation to go and serve at the Church of Today (which is now called Renaissance Unity) under the Senior Minister, Jack Boland. Jack invited me to speak at his church in Warren, Michigan, and I went and had a wonderful time. They wined and dined me, and then Jack extended a generous offer to come and be an Associate Minister there. The offer included an enormous salary, a clothing allowance, a luxury automobile, and a condominium on the lake. It fit all of my prosperity pictures of who I was as a minister. But the "go" signal wasn't there.

Jack kept telling me, "I need an answer," and I would say, "I haven't received my guidance yet." I had made a commitment to follow the will of God, and I didn't know what that was yet.

Finally, one day, we were at Unity Village (which is a community near Kansas City, Missouri, where Unity's international headquarters are located), and he said, "Edwene, I need to know whether you are planning to take this job because if you aren't, I need some time to interview more people."

"Jack, give me one more day," I told him. "I'll pray about it, and I'll let you know something tomorrow."

And so I went home, and I said to God, "Now, I really need to know something. Do you want me to go to Michigan? I'm willing to go, but you've got to let me know. Give me a sign and make it really clear."

That night, I had a dream. I dreamed of a map of the state of Tennessee. And in the dream a finger, like the big finger that reaches down from the clouds to touch Adam in Michelangelo's *The Creation of Man*, was pointing at the city of Knoxville. When I woke up in the morning, it seemed to me that the message was pretty clear. It didn't require a lot of interpretation on my part.

Well, I had never been to Tennessee. I didn't know anything about Knoxville. But I had made a commitment to follow God's will, and I had gotten a very clear "go" signal, so I knew what I had to do.

I told Jack, "Thank you very much. I am deeply honored for this invitation. However, my guidance is that I'm going to Knoxville, Tennessee."

He laughed. "What on Earth are you going to do in Knoxville, Tennessee?"

"I don't know, but that's where I'm supposed to go. So I'm going to have to decline your wonderful offer."

I went into the placement office to talk to the receptionist, Gladys, and I asked her to send my résumé to Knoxville, Tennessee. She just laughed.

"Honey, we don't have a church in Knoxville, Tennessee," she told me.

"There must be something wrong," I thought. "But I know I didn't misunderstand the signal; it was so clear."

I gave up trying to figure it out and went to lunch. When I came back, Gladys told me, "Edwene, you are not going to believe this! We just got a call from a study group in Knoxville that is looking to hire a minister."

"Well, send my résumé over there," I said.

I went to Knoxville to meet the study group, and they were wonderful folks. The problem was that they offered me only housing and $600 a month, which didn't fit my prosperity pictures at all.

"I really don't know what I'm supposed to do here," I told them. "I really needed more guidance. I don't think I can live off $600 a month." (I mean, my monthly dry cleaning bill alone is almost that!)

"Here's one of our cars," they said. "You drive on up into the Smoky Mountains and spend the night up there and get your guidance. We'll meet tomorrow, and you can tell us what you've decided to do."

So, I took their car. I had another person with me, and

we drove up into the Smokies. The mountains were just gorgeous.

"I'm willing to go to Knoxville if that's what God's plan is for me," I told my traveling companion. "But I need a sign. I need a better sign than just that dream. I need an absolute sign that I'm going to Knoxville, and that's what God wants me to do."

"Well, what do you want?" she asked.

"Moses had a burning bush, and I'm just as good as Moses," I said. "I want a burning bush! God, if you really do want me to go to Knoxville, Tennessee, you'd better give me a burning bush, or I'm not going!"

Just after I'd said this, we passed a small sign on the side of the road.

"Wait! Wait! Back up," I told my companion. We backed up and saw that the sign read, BURNING BRUSH NOT PERMITTED.

"Well, that's not good enough, God," I said. "It's got to be a burning bush, or I'm not going!"

My friend laughed. "Well, you certainly know what you want."

We kept driving, and suddenly I said, "Boy, wouldn't it be funny if we drove around this upcoming curve and there was a great big billboard that said, 'burning bush'?"

We drove around the curve and there was an enormous billboard that read, BURNING BUSH RESTAURANT, GATLINBURG, TENNESSEE.

Needless to say, we were absolutely stunned. In fact, we were so shocked that neither of us could speak for several moments. We went to the Burning Bush Restaurant for dinner, and then I accepted the $600 a month offer and moved to Knoxville.

I learned so much during my time there. First of all, I learned once again that the tiny paycheck the church gave me was not my source. God was my source. I had forgotten that my life was not limited by the salary I earned. While I lived in Knoxville, God provided for me in miraculous ways, and I had a rich and abundant life far beyond the means of my small paycheck. Plus, the people I worked with were just amazing; they taught me the true meaning of love. In all, it was a wonderful, life-changing experience, and I'm so grateful that God sent me such clear signs and that I had the good sense to follow them.

GETTING THE "STOP" SIGNAL

When you have made a commitment to do something, you may get a go signal that lets you know you're moving in the right direction. Then again, you may get a signal that lets you know you're barking up the wrong tree.

It was my lifelong dream to own a retreat center. Finally, after years of tithing and goal-setting, I was in a financial position to buy some land and start building. It was very exciting. And then I found some property for sale that was perfect. I knew as soon as I saw it that it was meant for my new retreat center. I made an offer, and my offer was accepted.

But then there were some problems. The first time I went to close the deal, it turned out there wasn't a clear property line, and they had to do more surveying. I thought, "Okay, we'll get this sorted out, and then we can move forward."

So they got the matter of the property lines sorted out, and I went back to close, and then it turned out that they did not have a clear title. They said, "Go ahead and sign, and we'll get this cleared out later."

I said, "Uh uh, I don't think so. I want you to get this cleared up first, and then I'll sign."

So they got the title sorted out, and I went back a third time to sign, and it turned out that the owners wanted to take 15 acres out of the parcel. And at that point I said to myself, "You know, I think God is probably trying to tell me something. I am not going to be pigheaded about this. I'm going to back off and pray and see what happens."

Just a few days later I was out antiquing, driving around in my van that could carry any antiques I bought. And I saw a sign on the side of the road: FOR SALE BY OWNER.

There was a one-lane country road, and I drove down it, way down into the boondocks. Then I went around a corner, crossed a creek, and came across a patch landscape that was absolutely breathtaking. It was just gorgeous. I mean, I had thought the first property was beautiful, but this was a hundred times more beautiful. I bought that land and built a retreat center on it, and now I cannot imagine being anywhere else.

So now if things don't seem to be going the way I wanted them to, or how I planned them to, I try to step back and say, "I'm probably being protected here."

COMING UP AGAINST
THE "SECOND FORCE"

After you have set your commitment, you may get a clear stop signal, at which point you should pull over and reassess the direction you're traveling in. Or you may encounter something else, which might look and feel like a stop signal but which is actually something else entirely. Occasionally, when you take a new step, when you set a goal or embark down a new path, the universe may send along something to kind of test you to see if you really mean business. Peter Oespensky, a Russian metaphysician, called it the "second force." (In the old fundamentalist church, that is what we call "the Devil.")

Not too long ago, I came up against a second force myself. I had the chance to witness someone throwing what I would call "an old-fashioned hissy fit." (And it wasn't me, thank God.) This person was ranting and raving and carrying on and throwing things, and as I watched this taking place I thought, "That's not really very attractive." And I knew that I myself had done that very thing, more than once. Many more.

So I decided to make a new commitment. I decided that I was no longer going to have upsets. Upsets were no longer a part of my life; I did not have the time nor the energy to waste on them.

Now, not long after I had made this new commitment, I had been traveling, doing my workshops, and finally it was time to go home, which is always a good feeling. I checked my bags at the airport, I had my boarding pass, I went to wait at the gate to get on the plane, and I was thinking about how good it was going to be to get home and see my dogs and have a chance to be in my own sweet, familiar home.

Then, using the loudspeaker, the airline employee behind the desk made an announcement: "Ladies and gentlemen, we are so sorry, but this flight has been cancelled."

Well, what do you do when you're not having an upset? I had no model for this kind of behavior. Everyone else around me was having an upset. They were cursing, and throwing things down, and yelling into their cell phones, and saying ugly things about the airline employee's mother.

I was just observing, thinking, "I am not going to have an upset." A group in front of me had gathered to grumble about how awful this was, and I thought, "What is my role here? What should I do?" I decided that my role was to bring a little humor to the situation. So I moseyed on up to the group and kind of inserted myself into the circle, pretending I was a member of it, and I waited until there was a pause in conversation, and then I said, "You know . . . if there is going to be a cancellation, I would so much rather that it happen on the ground than in the air, wouldn't you?"

Well, none of them thought that was funny at all.

Through it all, I admired the airline employee, who was being so gracious and diplomatic to all the people who were coming up with their anger and frustration. People were being so ugly with her, and she was giving back nothing but kindness, saying, "I'm so very sorry this is happening, and I will do everything humanly possible to get you where you need to be." It was beautiful to watch.

Well, I stood in line to get put on another flight, and when it was my turn to speak to her I said, "I just want to compliment you for your grace under fire. You're handling these people with so much dignity. I just want to thank you."

She said, "I hope you still feel the same way about me, Ms. Gaines, when I tell you that there isn't another flight out of here for you for the next twelve hours."

So I was just learning a whole new set of behaviors all day long that day!

I thought, what on Earth am I going to do for the next twelve hours? I had already turned in my rental car, so I couldn't go off on a drive. Remembering my commitment to stay calm and balanced, I thought I'd better pick something nice and relaxing. What would be nice and relaxing in the middle of an airport? I finally went to the newsstand and bought a no-brainer mystery novel. Then I found a quiet corner table in a restaurant. I took my shoes off, put my feet up, got my mystery out, and ordered a glass of Baileys.

During that day, I met many interesting people, enjoyed conversations with strangers who became friends, and passed several pleasant hours reading and relaxing and refusing to complain. I began to understand what it means to practice the presence of God in whatever situation I might find myself.

WORKING WITHOUT A NET

Sometimes, when you make a commitment with no way out and then you act upon it, it can feel like you're working without a net, and that can be scary. You have to take a leap in the dark, trusting that God has sent an angel to catch you.

There's a Scripture in the book of Job that says, "Thou shalt also decree a thing, and it will be established for you, so light will shine on your ways." (Job 22:28) Isn't that beautiful? You decree it, and then it is established. Light will shine on your ways, and you will know what to do. You will be given the understanding heart that knows what the next step is. But at the start, before you really know, it can be scary.

When I started my first success counseling business, I was very poor. But I was also totally committed to teaching prosperity and success seminars. I had $100 to work with, which was a lot of money for me in those days. Really a lot. I rented the Veterans of Foreign Wars Hall in my little community for $75. With the leftover $25, I took out a small ad in the local paper that said I was going to teach a class in self-awareness that would cost $10 a person. And then that was it. I had used up all my resources; I had nothing left.

I told God, "If I just recover my investment, I will consider this my go signal to continue." So on the night of the class I went early and cleaned up the VFW Hall. I mopped up the beer spills, swept up the cigarette butts off the floor, and got the room all ready. I was terrified that nobody was going to show up and that the $100 I had invested would be wasted.

Then I decided that if just one person showed up, I was going to do for him or her what I would do for a full house, because I had made a commitment to teaching the truth, and the truth will do its work, whether people are there or not. If you teach the truth, the stones will rise up and celebrate God! I decided that I was bigger than the little girl inside me who was scared no one would show up for her tea party.

Well, what ended up happening was that 55 people showed up, each with $10 in their hands. I couldn't believe it. After my $100 investment, I had netted $450 and, boy, that was a fortune in those days. It really got my new business off the ground. I took the money and rented the best office space I could afford for one month. It was really nice, with beautiful carpeting on the floor, and huge windows that overlooked Main Street. I took my mailing list of all the people who came that first night and wrote them a note saying that I was going to hold another class in my brand-new office space.

The problem was that even though I had this pleasant space, I didn't have anything else. I didn't have a telephone or a desk. And I didn't have any chairs for my students to sit in. And I'd spent all my money on the rent.

I sat on the carpeted floor of the office and explained to God that I had to teach a class in two days, but I didn't have any chairs for my students to sit in. I added that if we had to, we could all sit on the floor, and I would teach the class that way, because I was absolutely committed to teaching it, but it really would be nice to have some chairs.

Once I say a prayer, I always feel much better. I have made the Boss aware of a problem, and once the Boss is aware of a problem, I can trust that it will be handled. (Maybe not on my personal schedule, but it will be handled.)

Well, just a moment later there was a knock on the door. It was the custodian of the building.

"Welcome!" he said. "I know you'll be happy here." Then he looked around the empty space. "I saw in the paper that you have a class coming up Wednesday night," he said. "Where are your chairs?"

"They're on order," I said. After all, I'd said my prayer.

"Well, I've got a whole bunch of chairs in the basement you can use until they get here," he told me. "Would you like me to bring them up for you?"

I really do believe in angels. And I also believe that you can absolutely trust God with any matter, no matter how big or how small. But you must be 100 percent committed to what you're doing. Remember, I was going to teach that class even if everyone had to sit on the floor.

Wonderful, magical things can happen if you are willing to commit to putting yourself out there, stepping outside your comfort zones, playing at the game of risk. It feels like risk. It feels like playing without a net. But when you make a commitment, you're never playing without a net—because God is your net. Taking risks and acting on your commitment reduces you to simply trusting God.

YOU HAVE TO LEARN HOW TO SERVE

If you have made and verbalized a commitment and gotten a go signal but things aren't taking off in quite the way you'd hoped, perhaps the next step is that you have to learn how to serve. If you have not learned to serve in an enormous way, you are not going to be able to lead in an enormous way. This is a lesson I had to learn myself, the hard way.

Back in the 1970s, when I was in ministerial school, I already knew everything I needed to know; no one else knew that I did, but I knew it. I decided that I was going to start teaching. So I arrived at Unity Village, and I started going around to all the churches in the area, saying, "Hi. I'm here, and I'm ready to teach." Everyone laughed at me, because *all* the ministerial students wanted to teach when they got there, and the churches in the area were overwhelmed with people offering to do it.

I was annoyed that no one wanted my services. I continued to offer my brilliance, but no one threw down the welcome mat the way I thought they would. So I prayed about it. And finally I got the guidance to go to the church that was nearest my home. Instead of going in and offering to teach, I went in and I asked the minister, "What do you need doing? What is it that you need in this ministry?"

"What I really need is somebody to come in on Saturday and mop the floor," the minister told me. "And to come in early on Sundays and fold the bulletins and make the coffee."

"I can do that," I said. And I did. Every Saturday and every Sunday I would mop the floor and fold the bulletins and make the coffee. I did it week after week after week after week.

Nobody said, "Thank you." Nobody even noticed that I was doing it. But the funny thing that happened was that the more I did it, the more I began to love doing it. And as time passed I began to find more and more things that needed doing, like putting toilet paper in the bathrooms, making sure the cobwebs were off the ceiling fans, and cleaning up the mess the kids made when they ate snacks and drank Kool-Aid. I was doing all of these little things that no one else noticed needed doing, and I was totally enjoying myself. And I kind of forgot about teaching. (Once you learn the joy of giving and serving, that's what happens. Serving is no longer a chore or a burden; it's a joy. Albert Schweitzer said, "I don't know what your destiny will be, but this one thing I know: The only ones of you who will be truly happy are those of you who have sought and found how to serve.")

> "Each of us has a fire in our hearts for something. It's our goal in life to find it and to keep it lit."
>
> —Mary Lou Retton

Then, very early one Sunday morning, at about 6:30 a.m., I got a telephone call from the minister.

"Edwene, I've got laryngitis," she whispered. "Would you go in and teach the adult Sunday school and do the service this morning?"

That was far more than I had ever signed up to do. I never expected to actually do a church service. I just wanted to teach a little class. But what happens is that when you show the universe that you really mean that you are here to serve—and not just to get your name in lights and get all the glory, but you're really here to serve from a heart space that says, "God, I really want this world to work for every-body!"—when you come from that space, the universe knows you're finally ready. In other words, when you get to the point that you have the humility to mop the floor and fold the bulletins, and that you actually, genuinely enjoy doing it, suddenly you don't have to do it anymore.

A COMMITMENT TO GREATER SELF-LOVE

While you're making commitments to achieve prosperity and to serve and to do good in the world, why not also make a commitment to love yourself more? If you love yourself, other people will find you extremely easy to love. And people really do want to love you; give them the least little possibility of loving you, and they will. Wouldn't you like that? Of course you would. Each one of us would enjoy more love in our lives.

So how can we increase loving ourselves? What kind of a commitment do we need to make in order to increase our ability to experience self-love? One way is to cut loose and have fun.

Earth is the party planet. Did you get that memo? Earth is the party planet, so as well as doing our work and saying our prayers we also have to have fun. I myself enjoy walking with my dog in the woods. I let him run around off leash, and I watch him jump and play and explore. That's fun for me. That's the way my soul is fed. I like to take bubble baths. I like to read mysteries. And once in a while, I like to watch a really good movie or television show.

So, what is it for you? In what ways can you have fun and show love to yourself? Every day, you must set aside a portion of time for yourself. Every day! Because if you don't, you're going to store up all your tension and stress and then when you actually get a chance to relax, like on a vacation, you won't be able to.

As you make new commitments, make sure that one is that you do something special for yourself every day. And you must be clear about what that is. Name several things that you might want to do. "I want to read a novel for 30 minutes a day." Or, "I want to do my sculpture every day." Or, "I want to learn gourmet cooking." Or, "I want to work on my golf swing."

Whatever it is that you really love, schedule it in. As you do engage in activities that pleasure and feed you, you're going to find that you have so much more to give—so much more time, so much more energy, so much more attention to give to your children and your loved ones and your family and your church and your world. If only you will honor and accept and appreciate and take care of your own sweet self first.

There is an episode in Scripture that I think is a powerful lesson in self-care. It takes place after Jesus had been out walking on the hot sand all day, working hard and talking and teaching. At the end of the day, everyone has gathered to rest. Jesus was tired, and perhaps his feet hurt.

A young woman came along, and she began to rub Jesus' tired and aching feet—who knows, maybe she was doing a little reflexology. Then she began to pour some expensive oil on his feet while she massaged them, and it must have felt so good after that long day of walking in the hot sand. You can almost imagine Jesus closing his eyes, putting his head back, and saying, "Mmm . . . that feels good."

Well, Judas, the money carrier— Mr. Tightwad—came along and said, "You know, that oil is expensive, and we could have sold it and given the money to the poor."

Now this isn't in the Scripture, but I'm pretty sure Jesus said, "Well, you just hush your mouth!"

Jesus said, "The poor will be with you always." (And that's a statement I struggle with, because there will always be poor people in the world, no matter how much we give and do for them.) "But you will not always have me."

And I think that's a powerful teaching for us to be good to ourselves. There's always going to be a way for us to do good things or to spend our money to help other people, and we will do it. But not at the neglect of ourselves. The world will not always have us! One day we'll be gone.

The teaching is that we must love our neighbors as we love ourselves. Well, you cannot love your neighbor if you do not first love yourself. We have to learn how to take good care of ourselves. You have to be a being of integrity and do what needs to be done to make you feel whole and safe and complete and good. That's part of your job, as a child of God.

AN EXERCISE: TWO WEEKS OF SELF-CARE AND INTEGRITY

The most important commitment we can make is to ourselves and our own well-being. The fourteen tasks that follow are all life habits of self-care that invite prosperity. I encourage you to commit to making them a regular part of your life, starting with a two-week exercise. Each day, incorporate the next step into your life by taking deliberate action while continuing to practice those that came before. The longer you keep practicing these tools of self-care and prosperity, the more they will become second nature to you.

DAY 1: STRIVE FOR ORDER

The mystics tell us that order is heaven's first law. And it should be ours, too. We can never feel we're at our best when we're surrounded by a mess.

Today, take one step toward cleaning out all the clutter in your life. Tidy your house, balance your checkbook, file your paperwork, organize your office, complete any unfinished projects that have been weighing on your mind, clean out your closet, or get your car washed.

We can achieve order and harmony in every aspect of our lives with a habit of neatness. And when we de-clutter our lives, we signal to the universe that we are ready to handle more good.

DAY 2: TAKE TIME FOR SOLITUDE

It is in the quiet times of reflection and contemplation that we open ourselves to rich ideas.

Today, give yourself the gift of some time alone. We must all have a habit of solitude, regularly spending time alone in the silence by taking a walk in the woods, sitting on a hill and watching the setting sun, or simply taking a long, hot bath. Remove yourself from the maddening crowd and give yourself the opportunity of experiencing the quiet, gentle goodness of life. Refresh and recreate yourself in peaceful solitude and observe with wonder the amazing possibilities for your life.

DAY 3: CREATE BEAUTY

Always seek to create beauty in your environment. Today, take a look at your workspace. Is there anything you could do to make the space more inviting? Replace a worn-out carpet. Add a plant or a vase of flowers. Or, if you'd like to focus on your home, you could hang artwork, put bright throw pillows on the couch, or display family treasures.

We should all make beauty a habit. Strive for beauty in your person, too. Dress well. Get a good haircut. Buy new shoes.

Notice all the beauty in your life and thank God for it.

DAY 4: GIVE YOURSELF A TREAT

The universe will only treat you as well as you treat yourself. That means you must be especially good to yourself.

Today, think of one thing that you'd really love but that you "don't have time for," and then make the time. Get a massage, go to lunch with a friend, play a sport that you love, or practice a hobby that you enjoy.

Life is meant to be enjoyed. The better you treat yourself, the better you will find life treating you.

DAY 5: TELL THE TRUTH

Practice living and speaking from your sense of authenticity. Make it a habit not to hedge the truth, or to speak in half-truths. Be someone that others can trust will tell the truth about who you are and what you feel, because when you tell your truth with love, you empower others to live from truth as well.

Today, think of a recent moment when you did not tell someone the truth, or did not tell the whole truth. Now, go back to that person and tell the whole truth.

DAY 6: LAUGH

We celebrate God by finding the humor in life, so make it a habit to find opportunities to laugh. Today, watch a comedy or listen to a funny tape while you're driving to work. Read the comics in the paper. Go to the park and listen to children's laughter as they play. Make faces at yourself in the mirror.

God made the world a funny place, and you glorify God when you laugh.

DAY 7: REMAIN CALM

We can maintain composure even in trying situations by holding onto the firm belief that God is our source.

Today, face head-on a challenge you've been avoiding and keep your cool while you do it. Write your neighbor a polite note about his barking dog or calmly request a meeting with your child's difficult teacher.

When something unfortunate happens—a fender bender, a broken window, a chipped tooth—and you don't know how you will fix the situation, don't panic. Make it a habit to remain calm and to say to yourself, "All is well. God provides."

DAY 8: ACKNOWLEDGE OTHERS

Make sure that you notice and appreciate others and their contributions to your life. Today, choose a few people who have made a difference in your life and tell them how much they mean to you. Let them know your life is better because of them.

Make it a habit to give genuine and public compliments. Thanking people in public confers a double blessing. Everyone wants to be appreciated and acknowledged. Be a public appreciator and watch others light up with gratitude.

DAY 9: OPEN YOUR HEART

Try to make it a habit to allow everyone inside your heart space. Pay attention and notice when you find yourself feeling dislike toward someone. Ask yourself, "What am I avoiding in my own life by refusing to allow this person inside my heart?"

Today, choose one person whom you've had some negative feelings about in the past and try once more to open your heart to him or her. Remember, if you choose to love only perfect people, you will be a very lonely soul.

DAY 10: FEED YOUR SPIRIT

Today, do something consciously and intentionally to feed your spirit. Read an inspiring book or meditate on a favorite quote. (I've sprinkled my own favorite quotes throughout this book. You'll find a list of some books I've enjoyed on page 217.) Listen to a nurturing tape or attend a class or worship service. Take time for prayer. Sing a favorite hymn or listen to devotional music.

Make it a habit, each day, to turn within and ask for guidance as to what would feed your spirit—and then do that thing.

DAY 11: WELCOME CHANGE

Life does not stand still. It keeps moving and shaking. Just as soon as we think we've got our ducks in a row, change occurs. And when it does, it's a waste of time to worry, blame, feel guilt or disappointment, or practice any other negative behavior. It's much better to instead ask, "What new opportunities will this unexpected change create?"

Today, think of a recent change in your life that has upset you or thrown you off balance and try to look at it in a new light. Open your mind and ask if there's any way it might lead to good down the road. If you call the change good, no matter what it looks like or feels like, it must turn out to be good.

DAY 12: LET GO

You have the authority to release from your life all those people, situations, relationships, objects, thoughts, emotions, and concerns that do not empower you. As a being that is growing and changing, you must let go of that which is no longer enriching your life.

Today, take a moment to sit quietly and take a thorough inventory of your life. Let go of any elements that are draining your energy and disrupting your peace of mind. Release the burdens of the past and begin anew.

DAY 13: DO SOMETHING NEW

We never know where life will take us. All it takes is one small step to launch a whole new set of possibilities in your life.

Today, learn something new, no matter how small. Learn how to pitch a tent, to tie sailors' knots, to bake bread, or to say some words in a foreign language you don't speak. You never know where your new knowledge may take you. Make it a habit to keep expanding your awareness and learning new things.

DAY 14: EXPRESS YOUR GRATITUDE TO GOD

Notice the good in your life and give thanks to God for it.

No matter how bleak a situation you might find yourself in, there is always something to be grateful for—the blue sky, the sunshine, the warm bed, the nourishing food, the encouragement of a friend.

Today, deliberately find a small gift that you might usually overlook and give God thanks for it. The more we notice the sweetness of life, the more the universe gives to us.

CHAPTER 9

FINDING YOUR DIVINE PURPOSE

At one time or another you've probably asked yourself, "What is the purpose of my life? What is its meaning? Why am I here on Earth, and what am I supposed to be doing?" Chances are, you work hard, whether you take care of a household or have a job outside of the home. Your days are filled with seemingly endless chores and tasks like getting the oil changed in your car and going to the grocery store. Perhaps sometimes, when you get tired or stressed out, life can seem like just one long and meaningless "to do" list with a bland retirement and a gold-plated watch at the end of it.

You may have a sense that given the right circumstances, you could do much more than you are doing now. Perhaps you long to make a real difference in the world, to assign meaning to your life, and to listen to the yearnings of your very soul.

All of the great and wise people who ever made a difference on planet Earth heard their souls' yearnings and chose a purpose for their lives. People such as Gandhi, Mother Teresa, and Nelson Mandela seem to have been driven by a self-defined purpose that they chose for themselves. Now, we often think of such people with a sense of awe and respect as if they were somehow different from us—better, smarter, more saintly, or more courageous. Sometimes they hardly seem human. But the truth is that the only real difference between you and those people is that they all seemed to have a clearly defined life purpose that they selected for themselves and then embraced with steadfast dedication and unshakeable determination.

You have that very same opportunity as well. Every single one of us has some special gift, some special interest, some special talent, some special way of impacting this world, so that it becomes a better place for everyone. You have the potential to live at the level of Gandhi or Mother Teresa. The question you must ask yourself is, "Am I willing to define, embrace, and hold fast to my divine purpose, prayerfully, persistently, and patiently?" If the answer is yes, then the impossible truly can become possible in your life.

Now, finding and following your divine purpose is different from setting your goals. A goal is a tangible desire with an end result, but your divine purpose is really a way of living. For example, a goal might be to learn to paint with watercolors, but your divine purpose might be to bring joy to peoples' lives through your art. Another goal might be to get a PhD, but the divine purpose would be to live in the world of the intellect, the world of ideas. Your goals have finite deadlines, but your divine purpose is something that you will be working with and growing with for the rest of your life.

Years ago, a teacher explained to me that if I wanted to fully realize my potential in this lifetime the first thing I had to do was look out upon my world (understanding that we all look out through our own consciousness to see different worlds) and notice all the things that need healing, or fixing, or transforming.

"The greatest thing is, at any moment, to be willing to give up who we are in order to become all that we can be."

—Max De Pree

Very frankly, in my world, I see a multitude of areas where we as a human family need to direct our attention, change our priorities, get rid of the systems and concepts that are not working, and begin anew. Just to name a few examples, I believe that some new thinking needs to be done about the way we take care of our children, treat the environment, feed the hungry, share with the homeless, and provide for the disabled, the elderly, the imprisoned, the hurt, the abused, and the lonely.

The task, then, my teacher instructed, is that after looking carefully at the world, we must pick out one thing that we feel needs transforming, something that would be fun for us to get involved in repairing, shifting, restructuring, fixing, and perfecting. Please note I use the word *fun*. This is not about martyrdom or great personal sacrifice. It is about focus, joy, and a sense of purposeful possible achievement.

Next, we must take a bold step and make a 100 percent commitment to "fixing" the problem we have identified, followed by devoting our energies, time, talents, skills, and money to transforming that one piece of the earthly puzzle. Even as you're working toward solving the problem, keep in mind that what is *really* important is not whether the problem ever gets solved; it's that you are working toward the solution with dedication and persistence.

We are children of God. But children eventually grow up. And the evolving and advancing you will do when you begin to live according to your divine purpose is part of that growing up.

When you choose your divine purpose, you are framing your life with meaning. You are also taking an important step in your spiritual development: to demonstrate to yourself that you are a divine being and to prove to yourself that you have the power to affect change—that you are bigger, stronger, more powerful, and more creative than you thought.

It was Emerson who said, "Oh Man! There is no planet, sun or star could hold you, if you but knew what you are." (Now, I know what he *meant* to say was, "Oh Woman! There is no planet . . .") There is nothing in the universe that could hold us, if only we knew our true power.

The questions that you will want to start asking yourself are:

- What one issue seems most important to me?
- What would be the perfect solution to this challenge?
- Can I visualize it and see it clearly in my mind's eye?
- Can I write a description of what it would look like if the transformative work were complete and perfect?
- What do I need to know/have/be in order to begin?

- Is it time to go back to school, read the books, study with the experts, or learn the realities of the problems from those who have gone before?
- Is it time to do the research, the investigation, and the questioning?
- What is my first step, and how soon am I going to take it?
- Am I willing to do what it takes?
- Will I commit to staying the course, working in integrity, and standing alone in my mission if necessary?

What did you come to Earth to do? Well, whatever the answer is, it's time to start doing it. Richard Bach, the author of *Jonathan Livingston Seagull*, said, "It's good to be a seeker!" And it *is* good to be a seeker. But, sooner or later, you must be a *finder* and share what you have found with your world. We have far too many professional seekers on this planet, in my opinion. What we need are more finders.

I invite you to make a new commitment to yourself: Realize that you were not put on this planet simply to work hard and pay your taxes, retire, and then die. That's not your divine plan. (Now, there are a lot of people in the world who would like for you to believe that that's your divine plan, but you know in your heart space that you are here for much greater things.)

We are here on this planet to discover and demonstrate our own divinity. Perhaps you have already discovered your own divinity, that you are a creation of The Divine, whether you want to call that God or Spirit. All the great and wise teachers who have ever lived have given us examples of how to live according to divine purpose. Jesus told us to go and bear much fruit, and by our fruits we would be known. A common interpretation of being "fruitful" is that we bear children, but I believe that there are many other ways to be fruitful in this world—by writing books that entertain, by making paintings that bring others joy, by being a loving friend, and by living a life that encourages and inspires. We need to find out what it is that we need to do to prove—not to the rest of the world, but to ourselves—that we are divine. We must ask, "What work do I need to do to bear fruit?"

JOY IS YOUR COMPASS

God has given us an inner guidance system to help us find our divine purpose. It is the part of us that feels joy. As you take your first steps in seeking your divine purpose, I encourage you to get out of the daily grind, take a little time in solitude, and really re-imagine yourself and your life. You must turn within and try to listen for that which you long to do, to the yearnings of your soul. You must trust the process: that you may not be able to see the end result right from the start, but that if you begin in faith and do what you love to do—whether it is planting flowers, or painting paintings, or building bridges, whatever it might be—that you are embarking on the discovery of your divine purpose. When you follow your joy, at each step there will be a growing process where you will be given the chance to play in a larger and larger arena. Every time you stretch yourself, you will get stronger and wiser and more courageous. In this way, divine purpose is a process and not an end result, and we are following divine purpose when we are doing that which brings us joy.

Running a business, shooting a basketball, growing African violets, making go-karts, baking cookies—anything you love to do, do it! Let's say you love to sing and think that maybe music plays a role in your divine purpose, but you don't know exactly how. Well, take a baby step. Start by joining a choral group, taking voice lessons, or leading the children's choir at church.

Some people are able to live according to their divine purpose while at work at their jobs. Perhaps they work for a charity or nonprofit foundation that does good in the world, so they can follow their purpose while supporting themselves financially. Or perhaps their divine purpose is to share beautiful art with the world, and they own an art gallery. But it doesn't *have* to be this way. Following your divine purpose may be something you do in the evenings or on the weekends, completely separate from your paying work. This is fine, too. It doesn't matter *when* you're doing it, just that doing it brings you great joy.

Maybe you *want* to follow your divine purpose and find your true joy, but you're not ready to make a large, dramatic, selfless gesture like joining the Peace Corps or adopting an orphan. Maybe, for example, you just want to make dollhouses. That's fine. Make that your divine purpose and have fun with it. It doesn't have to be something huge or lofty or self-sacrificing. It just needs to bring you joy.

A friend of mine loves to work with her hands and do arts and crafts. She started to make little bead prayer bracelets that they use in the Buddhist tradition. She made them simply because she enjoyed making them, and it was a prayer activity for her. She sold a few and gave others away. She called very recently to tell me that she had been called by a company that wanted to place a wholesale order, and she was just thrilled. And I believe that's how the process works. You start by doing, and then the world opens up a larger arena for you to play in, and eventually you move toward prosperity while you do it. My friend started by doing what she loved, and now everyone is blessed by her making those beautiful little bead bracelets.

Joy is a magnet. It draws more joy to it. And when you are feeling joy, you will naturally bring joy to other people, no matter what it is you're doing. And bringing joy to other people is always good.

Now, joy can come in many different forms. Perhaps you decide that because of an experience you have had, your divine purpose might be to help others who are going through the same thing. For example, perhaps you feel drawn to help people with their addictions, or to counsel those who have been through a trauma such as rape. In this case, the joy might be a quiet and abiding sense of satisfaction. Just because you're not having the kind of fun you'd have at a birthday party doesn't mean you shouldn't do a thing if you are drawn to it.

But don't feel you have to aspire to martyrdom. In its own way, building dollhouses is just as important to our world as counseling addicts, and if it's what you want to do, by all means please go ahead and do it.

MAKING IT UP AS YOU GO ALONG

What if there were no "supposed to" to life, no single way to live your life? Instead, what if it was all about *choice*—unlimited opportunities and choices based upon your soul's yearning, your soul's natural desire to grow, learn, unfold, and become the person you have come here to be?

Maybe you already know your divine purpose. If that's so, good. But maybe you don't know it and finding it is one of the main reasons you are reading this book. If so, that's good, too. Finding your divine purpose sounds so profound and difficult, but really it's very simple.

I have a friend who lives in Florida. On her business card she has her name followed by the initials MSU. I thought it was perhaps like an MBA.

"Why Katie," I told her, "I didn't know you had an MSU. I am so impressed." Then I asked, "What is an MSU?"

"Oh," she said. "That stands for Makes Stuff Up."

Your life means what you say it means. Nothing more, nothing less. The fastest way for you to find your divine purpose is to make it up.

Now maybe you thought that the Archangel Michael was gong to appear in your bedroom one night and reveal to you your role in the cosmic plan. Or that Moses would appear in your living room with your divine purpose chiseled on a stone tablet. And maybe this will still happen. But instead of waiting endlessly for an outside sign, we need to turn inward and bring it forth from inside ourselves.

The easiest way to make a plan up is to ask yourself, "What would be the most fun thing I could do with my life?" And *that* is your divine purpose.

I'll say it again: Earth is the party planet. We are here to have fun. If you aren't having fun with your life, you're not doing it right. The era of the Christian martyr is over. And what I want you to know about me is that you can totally count on me to be a part of the party.

OTHERS WILL OBJECT

Do you want to have fun with your life while living according to your divine purpose? It's a big commitment, you know. And the odd thing is that when you decide to start having real fun with your life, when you start living according to your divine purpose, there are going to be people who will not be happy about it. And it might well be your mama or your daddy.

My own sweet little father is 93 years old. He lives in Houston, and every cell of his Southern Baptist body knows with absolute certainty that women cannot be ministers.

I was invited to speak in Houston several years ago, and it just so happened that it was the weekend of my father's birthday. So when I was there, I threw a big party for him at the hotel. We had cakes and balloons and gifts. The whole family was there, and we all had a wonderful time.

"You know, Daddy," I told him at the end of the party, "I've been a minister now for well over 20 years, and in all that time you've never once come to hear me speak. I would be so honored if you would. Will you come and hear me speak tomorrow?"

He hemmed and hawed but finally agreed to come.

At the end of the Sunday morning lesson, the entire congregation stood as one body and gave me a thundering, standing ovation. It was wonderful.

After the service was over, I stood at the door to shake hands with people. There were a lot of people, so it took a long time, and the whole time I could hear my father, standing behind me and tapping his foot. Tap, tap, tap. Finally I was through greeting everyone, and my father came around from behind me. He stood in front of me and looked me in the eye and gripped my shoulders, hard.

"Please . . . please . . . forgive me," he said. "I did not know who you are."

There may be people in your life who don't know who you are. And you can't allow them to stop you from doing what you are here on Earth to do. You are on a divine mission, and you cannot be derailed.

LIVING WITH INTEGRITY

Part of your new plan to live in alignment with your divine purpose is to start living with integrity. The word "integrity" means wholeness, oneness, completeness, so, by my definition, I am living with integrity when the outside of my life matches that which I profess to believe. For example, if I profess to believe that God is love, and that I am one with God, and therefore I am love, then how can I wave an interesting gesture at someone who cuts me off in traffic? That would not be a gesture of love.

When you are a person living with integrity, you will meet all sorts of people who may not like you, or what you are doing. But let me let you in on something: You did not come to planet Earth to win a popularity contest. Instead, you came here on a mission. You came here to do something very important. You came here to live according to your divine purpose. And when you are doing the job you came to do, there are going to be some people who aren't going to like you. Can you learn to live with that? In order to be a being of integrity living according to your divine purpose, you are going to have to learn to be okay with who you are, no matter what some other people might think or say.

I had an interesting experience recently. There was a woman I would see at meetings that I attended, and I didn't like her. My experience—my judgment—of that woman was that she was very cold, aloof, self-important, and that she believed she was better than I was.

Then one day, that woman came to see me in private. And she said, "Edwene, I suffer from a serious and really terrible social phobia. Will you pray for me?"

Well, I felt about an inch tall. What had been happening while I had been judging this woman was that she was doing everything she could possibly, humanly do just to stay in the social situation and not run screaming from the room. But because she did not behave the way that I thought she should, I made all kinds of judgments that had nothing to do with the reality of who she was and what she was doing.

If you are going to live in integrity, then when you meet someone that you don't like or who hurts your feelings, you have to say, "I don't have a clue what is really going on with this person. I just have to love them and have to allow them to behave exactly the way they please." This has to apply to everyone: your boss, your spouse, your parents, the president of the United States—you name it.

AFFIRMATIONS FOR INTEGRITY

If you allow the following affirmations to be your reality, they will bring you into integrity. I want to acknowledge they come from Tolly Burkan, founder of the Firewalking Institute of Research and Education, where I studied. He says, "This is how you walk on fire, and this is how you walk through life."

I always pay attention.

What happens when you don't pay attention? You have a fender bender, your check bounces, or your lover leaves you and you had no idea there was even a problem.

You must learn to pay 100 percent attention, right here, right now, in everything you do, whether talking to your children or listening to a piece of music. When you do, your life will be transformed. While you're walking a high wire, you can't be distracted, wondering about whether or not you remembered to feed the dog or turn off the oven before you left the house.

When you pay attention to something, you become whole with it (the Eastern mystics call this "tantra"), and something you are whole with cannot hurt you.

I always tell the truth and tell it quickly.

Often we don't tell the truth because we say to ourselves that we don't want to hurt people's feelings. That's a lie. The truth is that we don't want others to dislike us.

The thing about telling the truth quickly is that it eliminates so many problems. Let's say that someone invites to you a party, and you know right away that you don't want to go. You don't want to say, "I wouldn't be caught dead at your party," so maybe you hem and haw and say, "I'll have to let you know," or "Let me check my calendar and get back to you." But that is not telling the truth quickly.

Instead, you might say, "Thank you so much for the invitation, but I have another commitment." That commitment may be to spend time working on your model airplanes or taking a long walk in the park. But that doesn't matter. It's a commitment, and you are telling the truth. Now, I'm not talking about Truth with a capital "T," or a painful or hurtful truth. I'm talking about telling your personal truth. (And it's okay to say, "I'm embarrassed to say that this is my personal truth right now.")

The longer you string people along, the more pain you inflict in the world. You must tell the truth and tell it quickly. To everyone. Even the IRS.

I always ask for what I want when I want it.

People often have this notion of, "If my wife loved me, she'd know what I want," or, "If my husband loved me, he'd know what I want." But that's not true. People aren't mind readers.

My ex-husband was always very good about taking out the garbage. It was kind of an unspoken agreement that he would do it. Then one morning I got up and saw that it was all piled up; he hadn't taken it out the night before when I thought he should have. He came downstairs whistling, with his golf clubs, and said, "See you later."

Well, all day I stewed about the garbage. I said to myself, "I'm not taking it out. It's not *my* job." All day long I rehearsed the argument we would have when he got home. It was a horrible day that I spent fussing about that garbage.

Well, my husband came home, and he had had a great day. He walked in, took one look at me, and asked, "What's wrong?"

Well, every woman reading this book knows what I said: "Nothing."

Folks, that is not telling the truth or telling it quickly!

When he came down in the morning, I could have said, "Honey, would you mind taking out the garbage before you go?" But because I didn't, I ruined a perfectly good day over some garbage. And that was not living in integrity.

I always take total responsibility for my experience.

How do you know whether you are doing this? If you can feel inside you any blame toward anyone else for anything, then you are not taking total responsibility for your experience. Learn to take responsibility for yourself and your life and stop blaming others for whatever pickle you happen to find yourself in.

It's crucial to understand that no matter what is going on in our world at any given time, we have the power to change it when (and only when) we are willing to take responsibility for it. The truth is that what life presents to you is a direct result of what you have presented to your inner self in terms of your thoughts, feelings, and actions. If you don't like what is going on in your life—accept responsibility for it. Then you will have the power to change it.

I always keep my agreements.

First, you have to know what the agreement is and whether it has actually been made. For example, with my first husband, I had assumed we had agreed to a monogamous relationship. Imagine my surprise when I discovered he had a completely different understanding!

It's a good thing to go over the agreements you have with the people you love, and then to honor them. Especially with your children. If you have an agreement that you are going to pick up your child from soccer practice at 5:00, that does not mean 5:02. (When you are late, the statement you are making is, "I'm better than you, and I want you to know that.")

Be clear about what your agreements are, and then keep them.

VISION STATEMENTS

A vision statement is something that I encourage people to do while seeking their divine purpose. First, you must take yourself outside your normal daily life. Some people may choose to go on a retreat, or perhaps you simply need to take a long walk or sit quietly somewhere where you can really think. Having done goal setting in the past, you are more tapped in to your wants and desires, and now is the time to really start thinking big. You might choose something really big and outrageous that there is no way you could do yourself, so you're really going to need God's help. And anyway, whether or not you achieve the thing is not the point. The journey and process of getting there is the point. It's part of your growth, part of how you fully develop into a divine being.

How do you envision your work and your life? The key word here is "vision"—something you can see. For example, on one of my early vision statements, I wrote out a dream of mine—to have a retreat center where people could come and reconnect with who they really are. I described it with its trees and rolling hills and the creek that would run through the property. This was more than simply a goal; it was mega-goal, a wild dream, a seemingly impossible desire of my soul that I would get great joy in simply working toward. Seemingly impossible, and yet today I live at that center.

Think about your soul's deepest desire, and then sit down and write about it. Merely writing out a vision statement is a powerful step forward in your spiritual development. I have seen it help many, many people. One of those people, a man named Bob, has graciously allowed me to share his story.

BOB'S VISION STATEMENT

Bob is a member of a New Thought Fellowship in Michigan. Bob was raised a Presbyterian, but he had left his church and did not have a faith life with an organized religion while he and his wife, Diana, raised their three children. Then, once Bob's children left home, he started to reopen his life to faith and explore his inner self.

During the same period of time, Bob had started the process of trying to sell the family business, which he had run for 25 years.

Selling a business is no easy process, and there are no guarantees. Months of negotiation can be put into a deal, only to have it fall through, and then the seller has to start all over again. And such delays and missteps can be costly. Bob and his brokers had already been in a negotiation with a larger company that expressed strong interest in acquiring the business and alluded to a possible $7 million offer, but suddenly and mysteriously, the prospective buyer dropped out of sight. Bob's brokers couldn't even get them to return phone calls. This reversal was deeply upsetting to Bob, who had invested a lot of time and effort moving the company's interests toward an actual deal. Bob's brokers said they had never experienced anything like it before and had no explanation as to what had happened.

After one of my prosperity talks at the New Thought Fellowship, Bob told me that he was fascinated by my beliefs,

which were completely new to him. Bob had always been rel-
atively prosperous, having worked all his life, earned a good
income, and amassed savings and retirement accounts, but
he was open to receiving more. Bob was ready to retire, but
he still had to sell the business before he could. He was faced
with having to start the sales process all over again.

Having listened to my talk, Bob immediately felt moved
to start the practices of tithing, forgiveness, and intention setting, concepts he immediately grasped and wanted to make
part of his life. Bob wanted to live even more abundantly and
understood that these practices were going to be key.

Looking back, Bob says, "These practices are among
the most joyful that I have ever done. In the time since
I've started them, they've caused great things to happen in
my life, but it really wouldn't matter if they didn't bring
about concrete change. I would do them anyway, just for
the joy of it."

Having understood and incorporated the first three
spiritual laws of prosperity, Bob was ready to embark on the
fourth—following his divine purpose. But he hadn't yet
decided what form that would take.

I mentioned to Bob that I was organizing my first all-
men's group, which would be held at my retreat center in
Alabama. The goal of the group would be to help men develop "vision statements" for their lives so that they could
start to live according to their divine purposes.

After much reflection, Bob decided to attend the workshop, one of the most important parts of which was writing
out vision statements—the great and seemingly impossible

dreams according to the yearnings of the soul. Bob's vision statement was made up of five parts, and one was that he wanted to start an institute that would support the spiritual growth of humankind worldwide. He decided that the seed money for the institute would come from the sale of his family company, so he also set an intention to successfully sell the company.

Back at home, Bob continued to do his tithing and forgiveness work, and he continued to develop ideas and plans for his institute. Two months later, he got a phone call from his brokers who said, "You're not going to believe this. We just got a call from the company that had originally been interested. They were falling all over themselves with apologies for not getting in touch, and they are begging to get back into negotiation." Bob's brokers were so incredulous at the unlikely turnaround that they were actually laughing while they told the story.

Discussion resumed and a letter of intent was drawn up. While the preliminary offer had been named at about $7 million, it had now gone up to $10 million, in part because of the other company's delay and bad behavior.

I had told Bob that we live in an exacting, detail-oriented universe, and that it might take anywhere from six to nine months before he would see results from his new spiritual practices. A letter of intent with terms and conditions of the sale arrived six months almost to the week after Bob had attended the workshop. The deal was signed and sealed almost exactly nine months after it.

Bob had been absolutely sure that the buyer company

was gone for good and believed beyond a shadow of a doubt that their return was a direct result of his commitment to his new intentions. Needless to say, at that point Bob became a true believer in the spiritual laws of prosperity.

Bob still has the vision statement he wrote back at the workshop, which he carries with him in his wallet. Now retired, with the proceeds of the sale of the company tithed on and now earmarked for his new venture, Bob has devoted himself and his life to working with his wife and a third party toward the realization of his dream of an institute to support the spiritual growth of humankind worldwide.

Bob's experience is a wonderful example of how the discovery of divine purpose takes place. He made a choice about what he had to offer the world while listening to the yearnings of his soul. Bob lives in alignment to his divine purpose, and with greater joy now that his life is framed with meaning.

UNEXPECTED PROSPERITY

Bob and his brokers were shocked when the buyer company came back and made such a huge offer, but looking back, I'm not all that surprised. After all, Bob had started playing in a much, much bigger arena, and the bigger you play, the more you get. When you're starting to live in alignment with your divine purpose, unexpected prosperity is going to start happening in your life. I can almost guarantee it.

There's an affirmation that the people who attend my workshops always enjoy: "Large, rich, opulent, lavish, financial surprises now come to me, and I am grateful!" I'm not sure where I first heard this affirmation. It may well have come from Catherine Ponder, who has given us so many wonderful prosperity teachings, and if it did, I thank her for it. In any event, it's an affirmation that I love, and the key word in it is "surprises." The fact is that you have no idea what is in store for you or how God plans to give you your good. (So if you're one of those people who has to know how everything is going to happen in advance, then you need to start getting over that right now.) Personally, there's nothing I love more than large, rich, opulent, lavish financial surprises. And I believe that God loves to give them.

About a year ago, I was invited to speak at three churches in Minneapolis. Because it was winter, I was worried about getting caught in a snowstorm. But I knew the people of Minnesota would know how to deal with the weather, since they have to deal with it all the time, so I put it out of my mind.

I went to Minneapolis, and what happened was that I didn't get caught in a snowstorm. I got caught in a tremendous ice storm that shut down the freeways and closed all the churches, and all my workshops were cancelled.

At the time, I was in a motor home, and I was starting to get frightened because I couldn't find an RV park to pull into. At all the parks the water systems were frozen, and they weren't receiving any more vehicles. Finally I looked through the phone book and found a little RV park about thirty miles south of Minneapolis that had one opening. And I said, "Please hold it for me, I'll be right there!"

When I arrived at the park, I saw that it happened to be located at an Indian casino. And I was able to park my motor home and get it hooked up so that I had water and electricity. I was very grateful to be safe and warm in the midst of the terrible storm.

Unfortunately, I still had a problem; I had a payroll to meet each week. The fact that I had traveled all this way but was not going to be receiving any money from these workshops had me concerned. So I prayed about it just to make sure that God understood the situation. And then I reminded myself that the workshops weren't my source; God was my source.

Once I'd finished my prayers, I wasn't quite sure what to do with myself. The Boss had been made aware of my problem, so there wasn't really anything else for me to do about it. And what do I do when I have nothing to do? I try to have some fun. But I wasn't quite sure how I was going to have fun in the middle of an ice storm, so I tried to think of an idea.

I looked out the window of my motor home, and I could see through all the weather the colorful neon lights of the casino, and I realized that despite the storm they were still open. And it seemed to me that that casino was probably my best chance at having some fun that day. So I bundled up and put on my snow boots, placed a bunch of quarters in a plastic baggie, and I went slip-sliding across the icy parking lot over to the casino. It was nice and warm inside, although there weren't many people in there because of the storm.

I went up to a machine that I had never seen before, a kind of a super lotto thing with a jackpot of $10,000. I played one quarter, and then I played another quarter. It was fun, but not much was happening. So then I decided I was going to be brave and play really big, and I put in *two* quarters.

All of a sudden, all hell broke loose. Lights started flashing, bells started ringing, and a siren went off. I was taken aback; I didn't know what was going on. Then I saw that I had hit every single number, which meant I'd won the jackpot!

The casino offered to give me a check so that I didn't have to worry about carrying around so much money, but I asked them to give it to me in cold hard cash, because I'd never seen that much money in bills. And it was a nice little stack of money.

Now, it was great to win a jackpot, but I had not gone over to the casino to win. I had gone there to play. There's a big difference. I knew that God was my source, and not the lotto machine, so I was just there to have fun. And then I was given a lavish financial surprise—believe me, no one was more surprised than I was when those lights started flashing and bells started ringing. And it *was* a lot of fun.

Say it—and say it like you mean it: *Large, rich, opulent, lavish, financial surprises now come to me, and I am grateful!*

A CALL TO CONTINUE
THE JOURNEY

Now that you've begun to live in a whole new way, you might start to realize how addicted you've been to guilt, fault-finding, criticism, and a host of other negative behaviors in the past. While the journey to prosperity isn't exactly like the process of overcoming an addiction to drugs, alcohol, or cigarettes, there are similarities. And like staying free from chemical dependencies, remaining on the right spiritual path may not always be smooth and free of challenges. After all, we're only human. And it doesn't help that we're surrounded by a culture that encourages many of the habits we are working so hard to avoid.

Ask anyone who's overcome an addiction, and he or she will tell you that while getting clean and sober is a great accomplishment, and may seem like an end goal, it's really just the beginning. True freedom requires that we be awake and aware, and we must choose constantly every day to stay on the right track and avoid slipping back into old ways of thinking and behaving.

In the future, you may come across stumbling blocks,

U-turns, setbacks, and temptations to revert to negative behaviors. This is normal and does not mean that you have done
anything wrong or that you have lost all ground and are back
where you started—even when it sometimes feels that way.

Before you read this book, you probably weren't living according to the spiritual laws, but now you are (or at least you
will very soon). And as a result, it's highly likely that your life
will take a big turn for the positive. You'll experience the joy
of tithing. You will have a greater sense of possibility through
goal setting. You will have greater peace of mind because of
your forgiveness work. Your life will be framed with meaning
because you'll have started living according to your divine
purpose. Maybe you'll find a romantic partner, start a new
business, experience new opportunities, and have new ideas.

At the same time, it may be that your life has suddenly
seemed to take a turn for the worse. Maybe a long-term relationship has fallen apart, or you've lost your job. When this
happens to people, they often come to me and say, "What did
I do wrong?" Well, the answer is that they didn't do anything
wrong. Remember, sometimes we have to let go of what
doesn't work for us to make room for the new good. Often an
event that may seem like a crisis in the moment is really a
blessing, but we can see this only when we've looked back at
the event years later. This has certainly been the case for me
many, many times. And each time I am reminded to trust that
God's will for me is good and only good, if I will just allow it.

When it comes to the important truths about life, we humans sometimes need to hear the lesson over and over again. At
times, I myself feel as though I've forgotten every wise and true
thing ever taught to me, and I feel that I've suddenly gone com-

pletely off course. When this happens, and I become really confused and despairing, I pray, "Please show me what to do here. I am lost again." And then I always have the great joy of being guided back, of feeling, "No—I'm not lost. I know what I need to do." And then I begin all over again with the basic steps—tithing, goal setting, forgiving, and living my divine purpose. And I will continue to keep doing this—going back to the basics and starting all over again, as many times as it takes.

When I first started my spiritual journey, I was looking around for the perfect guru, who would smack me on the head with a holy stick so that I would be enlightened once and for all. I was so disappointed when I finally realized that exploring my spirituality and deepening my faith was something that I had to do for myself, and that there was no "once and for all" about it. Instead, it is a lifelong journey, and how you create the world that you live in is not based on a one-time event. Instead, it is an ongoing, everyday process—one that requires you to develop discipline.

Now, a lot of people don't like the term "discipline." It sounds negative to them. But actually, discipline is a positive thing. I myself have loved the word since I learned that both "discipline" and "disciple" have the same root—the Latin term *discipulus* for "pupil," or one who learns. I myself continually seek to learn, and I urge you to do the same.

Thank you for taking this journey with me. Having read this book and starting to put the principles into practice, you have done a lot of work. You should feel very proud of yourself for coming this far on your spiritual journey, and I congratulate you for it.

You are not, however, at the end of your spiritual

experience. Instead, you're just getting started. I encourage you to continue your journey consciously and deliberately, deepening your faith and your sense of what is possible in your life and of how much good God has in store for you. I urge you to continue to elevate your life to one of faith, love, risk, integrity, commitment, persistence, gratitude, passion, and discipline—and to continue to abide by the four spiritual laws each day, as a lifelong devotion. Most of all, be prosperous! Accept all the wealth that you want for yourself, knowing it is your divine birthright.

Jesus Christ said, "You are the light of the world. A city that is set on a hill cannot be hid. Neither do men light a candle, and put it under a bushel, but on a candlestick: and it giveth light to all that are in the house. Let your light so shine before men, that they may see your good works and glorify your Father which is in heaven." (Matthew 5:14–15)

Let your light shine so brightly before men and women that they see God in you. And seeing God in you, they will know then that God is in themselves, as well. Let your light shine. Let it! You don't have to *make* it shine. You only have to *let* it shine.

You do that by being who you really are, with no act and no pretense. By being honest, telling the truth, forgiving yourself, setting your goals, tithing, acknowledging God as your source, and getting on purpose with your life. By keeping your priorities straight and reminding yourself that a life of prosperity is about far more than money. It is about experiencing joy, achieving your greatest possibilities, and being all that your Divine Mother-Father brought you here to be.

God bless you. You are the light of the world. Go forth and shine brightly.

SUGGESTED READING LIST

- Claude M. Bristol, *The Magic of Believing*
- H. Emilie Cady, *Lessons in Truth*
- Charles Fillmore, *Prosperity*
- Frances W. Foulks, *Effectual Prayer*
- Napoleon Hill, *Think and Grow Rich*
- Emma Curtis Hopkins, *High Mysticism*
- Mary Katherine MacDougall, "What Treasure Mapping Can Do for You" (a brochure published by Unity)
- Phillip C. McGraw, PhD, *Life Strategies: Doing What Works, Doing What Matters*
- Joseph Murphy, PhD, *The Power of Your Subconscious Mind*
- Catherine Ponder, *The Dynamic Laws of Prosperity* and *Open Your Mind to Receive*
- Florence Scovel-Shinn, *The Game of Life and How to Play It*